Alan Butler qualified as an engineer, but has spent the last 30 years immersed in the history of the world and developing an expertise in ancient cosmology and astronomy. He has written many books, the majority of which delve in the recesses of the past that often remain ignored. Under his own name he has published books such as *The Virgin and the Pentacle*, *Sheep*, and *How to Read Prehistoric Monuments*. Together with Christopher Knight he has co-authored four books, and other co-operative ventures include the acclaimed *Rosslyn Revealed* with John Ritchie.

In addition to writing books Alan is also an accomplished playwright and has created many plays for the stage and a number for national radio. He lives on the North Yorkshire coast of England with his wife Kate and, when not pounding away at the computer or travelling, he is to be found in his workshop, building musical instruments or tinkering with his ancient sports car.

Also by Alan Butler

The Bronze Age Computer Disc
The Warriors and the Bankers
The Templar Continuum
The Goddess, the Grail and the Lodge
City of the Goddess
How to Read Prehistoric Monuments

With Christopher Knight

Civilization One
Who Built the Moon?
The Hiram Key Revisited
Before the Pyramids

INTERVENTION

How humanity from the future has changed its own past

Alan Butler

WATKINS PUBLISHING

LONDON

This book is dedicated to the memory of Dr John Snow (1813–58),
who followed Sherlock Holmes' most famous advice, even though it had
not yet been written.

✳ ✳ ✳

Distributed in the USA and Canada by Sterling Publishing Co., Inc.
387 Park Avenue South, New York, NY 10016-8810

This edition first published in the UK and USA 2012 by
Watkins Publishing, Sixth Floor, Castle House,
75–76 Wells Street, London W1T 3QH

Design and typography copyright © Watkins Publishing 2012
Text Copyright © Alan Butler 2012

1 3 5 7 9 10 8 6 4 2

Designed and typeset by Jerry Goldie

Printed and bound in China by Imago

Library of Congress Cataloging-in-Publication Data Available

ISBN: 978-1-78028-526-9

www.watkinspublishing.co.uk

For information about custom editions, special sales, premium and
corporate purchases, please contact Sterling Special Sales
Department at 800-805-5489 or specialsales@sterlingpub.com

Contents

Acknowledgments

As always my heartfelt thanks go to my wife Kate, who helps, encourages and often even believes.

I'm always in debt to Michael Mann, who is much more than a publisher, and finally I offer a special award to my editor Shelagh Boyd, who has the knack of making a chore into a pleasure.

Introduction

Growing up as I did in the 1960s and 1970s, I was introduced to a raft of information that had become extremely popular at that time. The genre was heralded by the arrival of an author called Erich von Däniken. In 1968 Erich von Däniken published a book entitled *Chariots of the Gods*. The startling claims in this book made headlines across the world at the time, and rightfully so. He claimed that the path of humanity from its earliest emergence had been dramatically altered by the visitation to Earth of beings from other parts of the cosmos.

Whilst ordinary people flocked to read this book and the others that followed in its wake, orthodoxy was more circumspect. Von Däniken claimed there were many happenings, especially in the remote past of humanity, that could not be explained by normal means. 'How' he wanted to know 'could a fairly primitive Bronze-Age culture that existed in Egypt as far back as 2500BC have possibly built so many huge monuments?' Considering the limited technical abilities of the culture, it seemed positively incredible that structures such as the Great Pyramid, which contains an estimated two and a half million blocks of stone could have been planned and completed – apparently in very short periods of time. The ancient Egyptians were not alone in this regard. There are puzzles, such as the stones of Baalbek in Lebanon, where massive stone blocks, one of which weighs upward of 1,000 tonnes, were quarried and set in place at some unknown period in prehistory – representing a feat of engineering that would be hard to parallel today.

Meanwhile, across the Atlantic in Central and South America, other unknown cultures also quarried huge rocks without using any metal at all. They managed to fit them together like pieces of a massive jigsaw puzzle, so accurately that after countless centuries it is still impossible to fit a penknife blade between them. They produced great citadels that have survived the many earthquakes that regularly shake these regions, whilst colonial buildings left in the same area by the Spanish have crumbled to dust.

Using these and countless other examples, Erich von Däniken made a good point. He addresses those aspects of history that a fair proportion of experts would prefer to leave alone. Clearly nobody can deny that such structures exist – they remain on the landscape for anyone to see; yet when archaeology teaches us of the cultures to which these masterpieces of engineering are attributed, it seems incredible that our ancient ancestors, no matter how bright they may have been, could have had the resources, the manpower, or the incentive to manage such herculean tasks.

Erich von Däniken made what might still sound like a preposterous claim when he dared to suggest that ancient peoples had not managed many of these building feats on their own. Rather, he proposed that these societies had been infiltrated with beings that were far more advanced than humanity was at the time. Von Däniken claimed there was significant evidence that the Earth had been subjected to countless visitations of beings from other planets in the cosmos, and it was these visitors who had provided the means and also the incentive to plan and build some of the most impressive structures of the remote past.

He pointed to mythologies from around the globe, retelling stories of giants and super-beings from many different cultures, suggesting that visitations of gods or demi-gods may have been nothing of the sort. Von Däniken reproduced rock art and folk art in the form of costumes and masks, all of which seemed to speak not of mythical gods but rather of corporeal beings who had influenced many different civilizations.

Other writers looked at these puzzles, but came to different conclusions.

Some pointed to the stories of Atlantis, the lost civilization first written about by Plato, who claimed that Atlantis had been a great island that was to be found in the Atlantic, far beyond the Pillars of Hercules. Plato's Atlantis was in many ways the ideal civilization, but it had eventually grown corrupt and, because the gods came to despise it, the island was swallowed up in a series of earthquakes and volcanoes. Modern writers asked if Plato had been responding to much earlier sources and wondered if Atlantis, or some place like it, had actually existed long before the civilizations we *do* know about rose to greatness. Perhaps the influence of some now virtually unknown, forgotten culture was responsible for the apparent miracles from prehistory?

Faced with a deluge of interest in such matters, experts responded, pointing out obvious mistakes made by Erich von Däniken and other speculative writers of a similar sort. By so doing they sought to 'recapture' history for orthodoxy. In the main it did not work, and the truth is that there is much from the ancient past of humanity that still makes very little sense, at least in terms of the explanations trotted out by historians. To suggest that all the questions Erich von Däniken and others of his kind were asking are irrelevant, simply because a few of von Däniken's supposed solutions have been tested and found wanting, is not reasonable and is a classic case of throwing out the baby with the bath water.

For all manner of reasons outlined in this book, I never personally accepted the alien intervention theory as being at all likely. This is not to suggest that it is an impossibility, merely that I consider there are better and less complicated ways of addressing the situations outlined by von Däniken. Nevertheless, I have been sure from my early 20s, and have only grown more convinced in the decades that followed, that our common heritage is not what orthodoxy would wish us to believe. I look at many of these problems, particularly those associated with massive structures from extremely ancient times, with the eyes of an engineer, which is what I am. I focus my attention on the logistics and the mathematics of building the Great Pyramid or moving the giant stones of Baalbek and I ask myself whether the planning, the resources or the technical expertise necessary could possibly have been in place when these structures went up. In many cases the answer has to be a resounding no.

Nor do I restrict myself to events that have taken place during the long and tortured past of our species – which, after all, is not really that long. In terms of the age of the Earth, the era of humanity has been incredibly short. At most we can push our own species back 200,000 years, as against the 4.6 billion years that the Earth has existed. Even the very remote past contains puzzles that are difficult to solve. For example, how did life come to inhabit our small corner of the universe and, in particular, how did something as absolutely complex and incredible as DNA come into existence? Is the road of evolution from ape to man really as straight and uncomplicated as experts claim?

CHAPTER ONE

Shifting Stones – Shifting Paradigms

A couple of hours' journey northeast of Beirut, in Lebanon, is the beautiful Bekaa Valley. This area has always been fruitful and verdant, so it isn't in the least surprising that it became an important area for Roman occupation just before the start of the 1st century AD. The Romans knew a good thing when they saw one and, in any case, were only following in the footsteps of earlier settlers. As far back as Old Testament times, in the Bronze Age, the great seafaring culture of the Phoenicians inhabited the Bekaa Valley and placed there a temple to the god Baal. For many centuries a city existed in this region, known from ancient times as Heliopolis, but the most impressive site to be seen today takes its name from that same Phoenician god and is known as Baalbek.

The Romans may not have known they were coming to a place that had been occupied since time out of mind, but as far as modern archaeology can establish, the site at Baalbek has been in more or less constant human occupation for around 5,000 years – and no wonder. Anyone who has been to Lebanon will be aware that large areas of it represent some of the most fertile land in the region. Early farmers would have been naturally drawn to the place and it is the remnants of these Bronze-Age farming communities that have been found at archaeological digs in and around Baalbek.

The Romans were great builders, and were always keen to consolidate their hold on a particular area by creating structures of their own – the better to 'Romanize' the people they subjugated. Baalbek was no exception and in this beautiful location successive Roman emperors built not one, but several temples to their gods, in the main replacing structures that celebrated deities already indigenous to Baalbek.

What remains of the Roman temples, after centuries of warfare, the successive comings and goings of peoples through the area, and many earthquakes, is still impressive enough. Julius Caesar commenced the first Roman temple at Baalbek in 15BC when he began one of the most extensive religious sites ever created by the Romans outside of their own home city. The site gained great importance and retained it until the 4th century AD, when Christianity arrived and pagan sites such as Baalbek fell into disuse. However, the Roman ruins in Baalbek safeguard a badly disguised secret that attracted significant interest during the 20th century and which still captivates people to the present time.

It is beneath the ruins of the Roman temple dedicated to Jupiter that accepted history takes an unexpected and even an alarming turn, because the temple stands upon a massive stone platform that differs absolutely from anything ever created by Roman engineers and which is, self-evidently, of a much earlier period than the Jupiter temple itself. This platform is known as the Grand Terrace and is comprised of a massive outer wall, in-filled and supported internally by huge stone blocks. The base of the platform is built from gargantuan pieces of squared stone, carefully quarried and fitted together extremely accurately. Many of these blocks are as much as 10 metres in length, over 4 metres in height and 3 metres deep. It is estimated that such stones weigh in the region of 450 tonnes. Not all the stones used in the platform have yet been excavated, but on the west side of the structure, above the base stones, are three even larger examples. It has been suggested that these stones, known as the trilithons, have an average weight of a staggering 1,000 tonnes.

The temple of Jupiter is on sloping ground and the quarry from which the stone for the platform came is some distance away, further downhill and accessible by twisting paths. There is no doubt about the origin of the massive stones because at a quarry site less than a kilometre from the temple of Jupiter, two other stones are still to be found. One of these is an estimated 1,200 tonnes in weight. It measures 21 metres by around 4 metres, and although it was never moved from the quarry to be used on site, it represents the largest known stone ever to be cut from the living rock by human beings. The Pregnant Woman, as the stone is called, is a leviathan, and even today there are very few cranes in the world that could lift it.

If we look at the stones at Baalbek that were definitely moved from the quarry, we are still dealing with beasts of up to 1,000 tonnes. Somehow, in addition to being cut from the bedrock, these monsters were taken uphill, across rough country, and lowered into place with the greatest of care, ensuring a perfect fit with their neighbours. Archaeologists may wince at the thought of Roman engineers even contemplating such a feat, but engineers say it would still be as good as impossible, bearing in mind the topography of the site. If such a task could be performed today it would cost countless millions of dollars and would require a levelling of the site and the creation of massive plant specifically designed and created for the purpose. Nobody would even contemplate such an undertaking.

Standing 650 kilometres southwest of Baalbek is the one remaining example of the seven wonders of the ancient world. This is the Great Pyramid and it is located, with its two companion pyramids, on the Giza Plateau, just outside the modern city of Cairo in Egypt. For centuries the Great Pyramid, otherwise known as the Pyramid of Cheops or Khufu, was the tallest and certainly the most massive man-made structure on the planet. When new it was 146.5 metres in height and it covers a ground area of 55,000 square metres. This massive structure is composed of an estimated two and a half million blocks of stone, the average weight of which is 2.5 tonnes, though many are much heavier. The combined mass of all this masonry is an estimated

5.9 million tonnes. Quite understandably the Great Pyramid has attracted a good deal of attention and is one of the most popular tourist destinations in the world. To stand at its base and stare up in disbelief at the scale of the pyramid seems to be a rite of passage for anyone who is even slightly interested in our ancient past; I will never forget my first sight of the Great Pyramid, shining and shimmering in the heat of a desert day.

Unlike the stone platform at Baalbek, there is no mystery surrounding the builder of the Great Pyramid, or so orthodox history would have us believe. Most books on the subject will tell the reader that the Great Pyramid was created by the Pharaoh Khufu, who reigned in Egypt between around 2589BC and 2566BC and that it was built in a 20-year period during the king's reign over the Old Kingdom of Egypt.

Such statements are meat and drink to those individuals who retain a sense that the ancient history of humanity is not at all the way history books would have us believe, and with good reason. It does not take long, armed with a simple calculator, to show that either the pyramid took very much longer than 20 years to complete, or else the technology used to create it was way out of kilter with what we would think of as being possible for the Bronze-Age Egyptians.

It is generally accepted that the limestone blocks that make up the great bulk of the pyramid were quarried on the same plateau where the Great Pyramid and its companions stand. Indeed, a good deal of stone must have been shifted from the plateau simply to make a level base for the pyramids, though a natural outcrop was probably used as part of the infill for the base of the Great Pyramid itself. Hewn blocks were then created and assembled on site, with the interior passages and chambers of the pyramid being made as the structure rose from the bedrock.

Nobody denies that the human effort necessary to build the Great Pyramid probably exceeded that of any other structure that has ever graced our world, but archaeologists and historians are not engineers. If I had not seen the Great Pyramid with my own eyes, when I came to look closely at the figures

I would have said it was an impossibility, bearing in mind when it was built and how it was constructed.

If the assembled workers on the site had worked for 24 hours a day, 7 days a week, and through every month of the year, during the 20 years the pyramid was being created, it would have been necessary to put a new stone into place every 4.2 minutes. This alone seems ridiculous. As the pyramid grew higher the stones had be dragged up some sort of ramp, and the ramp itself could have eventually contained more material than the pyramid. Nevertheless, there had to be ramps in order to get stones to the place where they were required.

Let us suggest that it took a team of men an average of 1 hour to get each stone from the quarry to the place in the pyramid where it was required (though this is probably not at all realistic). With each new stone arriving every 4.2 minutes, at least 15 stones must have been on the move all the time. This might seem possible because if there were 50 men to a team, there would only ever be 750 men hauling stones at any one time. With two complete shifts for the 24-hour day, that would equate to 1,500 men hauling stone.

So far, so good, but we have to take account of the fact that something like 360 stones were being lifted into place in every 24-hour period. Each one of these stones had to be broken from the quarry before being shaped and then harnessed so it could be manhandled across the site. We need to bear in mind that ancient Egypt was a Bronze-Age culture, which had no iron or steel. Bronze is a very useful metal, but it is not ideal when it comes to making chisels to cut stone – even relatively soft limestone. Bronze chisels will definitely do the job, but they would have to be sharpened on a very regular basis. For every person chiselling rocks to shape, there would probably have been another two, sharpening chisels constantly to keep him supplied. It could not realistically be expected that one man could prepare more than a single stone in a day's work, so with 360 stones a day needed, that would be a total of 360 chisellers, together with 720 sharpeners, with 2 shifts needed per day, making a total of over 2,000 people needed to prepare stones. This of course does not include the many individuals necessary to hack the stone from the quarry or to get it from the quarry to the preparation site. If we estimated another 2 people per stone, per day, we need to allow for another 700 men or so.

We are already up to more than 4,000 workers required, but this is simply the number needed to cut stone and get it onto the pyramid. No matter what method was used to get stones from the quarry, a substantial amount of wood must have been required. Since there are no trees to speak of in Egypt, all of the wood necessary must have been brought from somewhere else – most probably Lebanon. This would have required a great many ships, with attendant sailors and people to transfer wood to the site and to create whatever sleds, rollers and scaffolding were necessary.

Back on site, people were needed to carry water, both for the workers and to prevent friction on skids and rollers. More individuals were required on top of the growing pyramid, to manhandle the regularly arriving blocks into place. Extra teams were almost certainly required to create ramps (which some experts have suggested would have contained more material than the pyramid itself). Smelters and blacksmiths were needed, to make chisels and other metalwork necessary. Specialists would have been essential, to make the larger pieces of stone for chambers etc. – many of which were brought from a much greater distance than the limestone, often by boat along the Nile.

The number is growing dramatically, but we must not forget that all these thousands of people had to be fed, so in addition to a virtual army of individuals baking bread, preparing meat and brewing beer – for themselves and everyone else – we also have to take account of the fact that the necessary grain had to be grown, cattle and sheep raised, land irrigated and so forth, simply to keep the workers alive.

The whole thing is preposterous. There is no doubt that ancient Egypt was populous, its farmers were efficient, and its potential for growing crops significant, but the economy simply could not have coped with the mass of individuals necessary to create a structure such as the Great Pyramid in 20 years without bankrupting the entire nation – and of course this is all assuming work could be sustained across 24 hours of each day and throughout the unbelievable heat of the Egyptian summer, neither of which is very likely.

The necessary muscle involved fails to take into account the stunning achievement of those planning and supervising the building of the Great Pyramid, which is a tour de force in architectural terms, bearing in mind the period during which it was built. It was extremely accurately placed onto the landscape, aligned as it was to the four points of the compass. Building such a huge pyramid shape, without the whole thing twisting and corkscrewing as it rose from the desert, would have been in itself a daunting task. Complex passages and chambers had to be built 'into' the structure as it rose and could not have been cut into the bulk once it was finished. Subtle, and only fairly recently recognized, narrow tunnels lead up from the so-called King's and Queen's Chambers, deep in the pyramid, to emerge high up its sides. These tunnels were carefully aligned, so that at strategic times they would point to specific constellations of stars and even to individual stars.

The Great Pyramid and its two companions – the only slightly less impressive pyramid of Khafre and the much smaller pyramid of Menkaure – were built in such a way that they represent an earthly version of the three stars of Orion's Belt[1] and it is becoming more and more obvious that none of the three pyramids was ever intended to stand in isolation. They represent not only a masterpiece of construction, but betray an understanding of the sky, of mathematics and engineering, out of all proportion to that previously attributed to a culture from this remote period of history. To deny that the ancient Egyptians could have built the Great Pyramid and its companions would be to ignore the evidence of one's own eyes. Quite clearly they were built, but the circumstances of their presence must certainly be very different to that put forward in the vast majority of history books.

Half a world away from the Giza Plateau, in southeastern Peru, is the city of Cusco; it marks the site of the capital of the Incas, a people who ruled a vast area in this part of South America, prior to the arrival of the Spaniards and their subsequent conquests. Much of the Inca city itself was destroyed during the colonial period, but there is a structure nearby that has survived in a much better state of preservation, primarily because its massive stones would have proved too large to move. This is the citadel of Sacsayhuamán, which was probably once part fortress, part temple and part ceremonial meeting place. Sacsayhuamán is in the Andean mountains and is a place of sharp inclines and deep winding valleys. It sits above modern Cusco, though only a proportion of the buildings it once contained are still to be seen there.

Near to the great plaza of Sacsayhuamán are three terraced walls, each massive in scale and comprised of stones that, at their largest, probably exceed 150 tonnes. What makes the terrace walls at Sacsayhuamán so impressive is not simply their size, because a wealth of other cultures across the globe managed to move large stones about, but rather the way they were fitted together. The Incas were great builders and they are known to have used a system of construction that probably evolved to deal with potential damage from earthquakes, but Sacsayhuamán is on a scale unparalleled by other Inca sites. Using this system, stone blocks do not simply sit one on top of another, but are locked together like pieces of a jigsaw puzzle. At the time of earthquakes these interconnections flex, but there are so many of them that a whole structure slowly falls back into place once an earthquake has subsided.

What staggers most people when they see the terraces of Sacsayhuamán is the sheer scale of the interlocking that has taken place here. One might be forgiven for assuming that such complex interconnections between stones would only be possible with some malleable substance such as clay, but at Sacsayhuamán the puzzle has been created using extremely hard stone, most of which was clearly dragged to the site, up and down precipitous slopes for many kilometres.

If I was staggered by the accuracy of the joints between stones in Egypt, what was achieved at Sacsayhuamán makes the Egyptian's accuracy pale into insignificance. It is literally not possible to fit a piece of paper between the terrace stones at Sacsayhuamán, and some of the stones are as tall as, or taller, than adults and just as broad.

Having born this in mind we now have to take note of the fact that the Incas were a Stone-Age culture. They possessed metal of no sort, apart from gold, which is useless for tools of any kind because it is extremely soft. So, in theory at least, not only were the stones carved with extremely smooth surfaces, they were also shaped into the multitude of curves, protrusions and indentations necessary to lock them tightly into adjacent stones – and all with nothing in the way of tools except other rocks. Clearly, stone mauls would work – many have been found at sites such as Stonehenge and Avebury in England – but they could hardly be termed 'precision tools' and I cannot see how, when using stone mauls alone, it would have been possible to produce some of the intricate, interlocking shapes seen at Sacsayhuamán.

In truth nobody knows when the terraces at Sacsayhuamán were created. There is no doubt that the Incas, who inhabited the site at the time the Spanish arrived in the 16th century, used the citadel for both defensive and ceremonial purposes. However, there is no more reason to suggest they also created it than there is to assert that Julius Caesar was responsible for the stone platform at Baalbek. The concept of dragging such large stones up from valley bottoms using only human power is astonishing enough, no matter how many people were available. But the idea that 100-tonne stones could be carved into intricate shapes without the aid of metal and then slotted together with the apparent ease one might use to construct with a child's building blocks, and all without any form of crane, is beyond incredible. I respectfully suggest that anyone who thinks that this is what took place might assemble a team of strapping young men and try it for themselves. When even small-scale reconstructions of the technique used at Sacsayhuamán have been attempted, the results have invariably been laughable.

Like the Great Pyramid and the platform stones at Baalbek, the terraces of Sacsayhuamán are a reality – there for anyone to see. We cannot doubt their existence, but it is certainly valid to ask whether the general explanations of historians, as to how these stones came to be where they are, are reasonable or even tenable.

These are just three examples out of the hundreds I read whilst growing up in the 1960s. Such mysteries were well in vogue at the time and have not been adequately explained in the intervening period. Where these mysteries had a material component I made it my business to simply not accept the descriptions or explanations of other writers, but to see these sites for myself. As I learned more about engineering, I spent countless hours trying to devise simple machines, working within the supposed technological capabilities of the people concerned, that they may have created for themselves in order to make their tasks simpler, and to explain some of the puzzles. I am well aware that is all too easy to assume that those living hundreds or thousands of years ago were less intelligent than we are. This is not the case. They were not limited by a lack of brain power, but merely because of a less advanced technology than ours. In many cases experimental archeology shows that our ancient ancestors could be more ingenious than we sometimes are today – but they still could not achieve the impossible.

There are some occasions, such as the ones I have mentioned, when it is not possible to reconcile what was achieved with the supposed capabilities of the people concerned. The only way forward is a change in paradigm. In other words, there has to have been an element involved about which we know nothing. In the case of the Great Pyramid the way forward might be to assume that its creation took far longer than history suggests, but such a notion seems unlikely and would do nothing to explain either the platform at Baalbek or the terrace at Sacsayhuamán. Realistically, in all three cases what is needed to explain the completion of the structures would be a far greater level of technical expertise than ancient history seems to permit.

This is exactly what many researchers and writers have provided. One of the first writers to tackle such thorny issues in a popular sense was Erich von Däniken with his book *Chariots of the Gods,* published in 1968. Erich von Däniken's book was an instant success, perhaps because it appeared to answer questions that seemed to have no other satisfactory solution. Von Däniken suggested that there had been constant interventions into the history of humanity and that these must have been made by extraterrestrial visitors to Earth. He claimed that evidence for these alien visitors was the very structures they had helped to create, together with myths and fables from around the globe of giants and benevolent demi-gods who had brought knowledge and help to cultures. Sometimes, he claimed, these visitations had catapulted formerly modest peoples into great civilizations, such as those of the Egyptians, the Sumerians of the Fertile Crescent, or the Olmecs of South America.

Once the genii of ancient mysteries was out of the bottle, it would not return, with the result that the 1970s and 1980s especially were replete with books of the von Däniken sort. Not all were necessarily carefully researched and even Erich von Däniken himself made more than a few gaffs, such as describing what could have been a large aerial photograph of a circular structure in the Nazca desert of Peru as a launch pad for extraterrestrial craft when the true object was, in reality, only a couple of metres across.

Erich von Däniken has had his detractors and his first book, together with subsequent titles on the same theme, have been well hammered across the years. Nevertheless, to dismiss everything highlighted and described by him on the grounds that he sometimes allowed his enthusiasm and imagination to get in the way of reliable evidence is neither reasonable nor fair. If only one per cent of the historical puzzles and anomalies brought to print by von Däniken and other writers in the same genre genuinely defy logic, there is still a huge mountain to climb in terms of truly understanding our ancient past.

As I have already suggested, Erich von Däniken decided at the very start of his writing career that the reason for all the historical anomalies he listed was there had been a component to human history that is definitely not accepted by those who make it their business to study the past. Von Däniken was certain that our world had been subject to numerous visits by extraterrestrial visitors from other parts of the cosmos. This, he suggested, was the true explanation for massive structures such as the Grand Terrace at Baalbek – they were planned and probably even constructed by entities whose own technological accomplishments allowed them to travel across interstellar space. He proposed that the individuals concerned would have possessed sophisticated laser-cutting technology for quarrying stone, and even anti-gravity devices for 'floating' massive rocks to their intended destination. He suggested that massive projects, such as the Grand Terrace at Baalbek, may have been specifically created not to impress the locals, but rather to serve some now unknown purpose for the alien visitors themselves.

Orthodoxy falls out with von Däniken and other writers who followed in his train for a number of different reasons. Principally, critics would probably accuse him of taking a sledgehammer to crack a walnut. If we watch a stage illusionist apparently sawing his assistant in half and then miraculously reconstructing her before our eyes, we do not immediately believe that the entertainer is some sort of god, with control over life and death. To adopt such a position would be irrational. We may not be aware of the 'specific' trickery that has been employed, but our common sense tells us that what we have seen was not what it appeared to be. We 'know' that there must be a simpler explanation.

Similarly, invoking visitors from somewhere else in deep space just because we cannot explain how a particular structure was erected, or on account of some vague reference to super-beings in an ancient story-cycle, would seem to be ignoring a wealth of other possible explanations that are simpler.

We have to ask ourselves how likely such a contingency would be? Despite many hundreds of books, films and documentary television programmes dedicated to the subject of extraterrestrial visitors, there isn't a single shred of truly hard evidence that they are here now, or have been here in the past. Everything available is circumstantial. Governments are accused of keeping the public in the dark regarding extraterrestrials, both historically and today, but it seems to be stretching credibility to assume that everyone concerned would keep quiet indefinitely. I try to keep an open mind, but I have also adopted a position in which I consider the simplest explanation to be the most likely.

To assert that there is no life anywhere in the cosmos except for here on Earth seems to me to be absurd. With an estimated 100 billion stars in our local galaxy alone it is ridiculous to suggest that the same conditions that prevail here do not exist elsewhere. On the contrary, bearing in mind how resilient life is, surviving as it does in every possible niche on the Earth, it seems likely that the universe is teeming with life. The real problems regarding any such life-forms visiting the Earth are ones of timing and proximity.

As Douglas Adams commented in his wonderful creation *The Hitchhiker's Guide to the Galaxy*, 'Space is big! Space is very big!' Even the nearest star to our own Sun is 4.24 light years away. To get this into perspective, even if one could travel at the speed of light, which physics at the moment says is impossible, it would take a spaceship over four years to get there. Because of the complications caused when one approaches the speed of light, time for the crew of the spacecraft would pass extremely slowly, whilst it would whizz by on the Earth. By the time the crew returned they might only appear to be a few months older than they were when they set off, but on the Earth, many centuries would have elapsed. Space travel has incredible implications!

As mentioned earlier humanity has only existed in its present form for about 200,000 years, which is a really short period of time, even in terms of the age of the Earth which has been around for 4.6 billion years – and the Earth itself is not particularly old in terms of the universe, which at the moment is estimated to be 13.75 billion years of age. All manner of highly sophisticated civilizations may have come and gone in various parts of the universe during such a long period of time, but the possibility of any one of them not only existing but being capable of long-distance space flight during our own recent past is negligible to say the least. And even if this were the case, such a civilization would firstly have to find us and then be interested enough to take a hand in our development.

It is all very, very unlikely; not impossible but statistically remote. Perhaps in the near future someone will come up with definitive proof that we have been visited by extraterrestrials in the distant past, or that they are still paying us visits today, but at the moment no such evidence exists.

Having said that, I will soon provide the reader with hard, irrefutable evidence that things have taken place within the time humanity has occupied the Earth that cannot be explained simply – structures such as the Great Terrace at Baalbek and the Great Pyramid included. There is absolutely no doubt in my mind that the history of humanity is *very* different than orthodoxy would have us believe, but I find it impossible to ascribe this in any way to visitors from elsewhere in our spatial backyard.

OK, so if there have been no extraterrestrial visitors, could it be that the history of civilized humanity goes back much further than we presently realize? This is a much more satisfactory explanation than visiting spaceships; after all, we are here, and in terms of humanity itself we have been here quite a long time. As far as we are presently aware the oldest civilizations worthy of the name go back to around 4000BC – and this is working on archaeological evidence from around the world. As I hope to show, even at this remote period there were people around who had knowledge of the Earth and its place in the solar system that was generally comparable with what we enjoy today. The problem is that the majority of what these truly ancient peoples knew seems to have been lost and much of it was not regained until the last century or so.

As a result, it might be suggested, and in fact has been suggested regularly, that prior to the first human civilizations of which we have evidence, there must have been a totally lost super-civilization. Maybe this was destroyed by some sort of cataclysm and left only fragments of its knowledge with which to seed the developing civilizations that followed it. In many respects this would make a good deal of sense. If people at the very extent of our historical knowledge were brighter than any that followed for many centuries, we might be looking at the random survival of knowledge that could not be sustained in small, widely dispersed populations. Devoid of its original cohesion and technological trappings, humanity gradually 'forgot' much of what it once knew.

How bright would such a progenitor civilization have had to be? The evidence I want to put forward indicates that at the very least it would have been something like the sophistication of our own civilization by the start of the 20th century. There is proof positive that 'some' people living at least 5,500 years ago were well aware of the absolute size and even the mass of the Earth, and that they had gone so far as to produce not one but two comprehensive measuring systems that were 'based' on the vital statistics of both the Earth and the Moon, and also upon the speed of light.

In some senses it might be suggested that, whoever these people were, they had to be more advanced than we are, even now. This is because we have simply adopted the remnants of what 'they' knew about the dimensions of things and turned them into a slightly creaky but workable model, whereas their systems were holistic, incorporating the measurement of time, space, distance, mass and volume. They were even aware of very sophisticated concepts such as that of absolute zero on the temperature scale, which was an inherent starting point of the temperature measuring system they created.

For the moment the reader will have to take my word for all of this, but as my story unfolds I hope to prove beyond doubt that any 'progenitor' civilization that could have existed must have produced its own Newtons and Einsteins, was technologically adept, and had probably even mastered local space travel at least. All of this is fine, except for one fact. There is no proof whatsoever that such a civilization ever did exist on the Earth prior to the Stone Age. In order to understand why this is the case we have to look at the world as it is today. If some huge cataclysm came upon us tomorrow, great enough to disperse and fragment society but not significant enough to destroy humanity, what would be left for any observer to see in several thousand years? The answer is that there would be plenty.

CHAPTER TWO

Civilization Past – Civilization Future

A
s we have seen, the greatest of the stones quarried at Baalbek weighs an estimated 1,500 tonnes. In terms of our own lifting power, even in the 21st century, this is about as big as it gets. Logically, if we were to construct the Grand Terrace today we would need a powerful mobile crane, and a little research shows that the Liebherr LTM 11200–9.1 is the most powerful mobile crane possessed by humanity at this time. It is indeed a beast, an 18-wheeled leviathan with a reach of 100 metres. Assuming the ground was relatively flat and that there was road access between the quarry site and the location of the terrace, this mighty machine could do the work necessary to recreate the Grand Terrace. Alas, there never has been a suitable road access for this monster at Baalbek and the ground is far from flat, but we do at least possess a mobile crane capable of lifting all the stones that were used in the structure – just. But even the Liebherr LTM 11200–9.1 could not have raised the largest of the stones, the Pregnant Woman, from its quarry site because its lifting potential is 1,200 tonnes.

That this particular stone is still where it was quarried bears testimony to the fact that whoever did manage to excavate the majority of it from the natural rock of which it was once part, had also surpassed their technical capabilities when it came to raising the stone. This is because it remains there to this day, at a somewhat strange angle, as if 'someone' tried desperately to raise it – but failed. To be fair, estimations of the true weight of the Pregnant Woman stone do vary, and some possibly overconservative estimates place it at a mere 1,000 tonnes, but even if this is the case it still weighs the same as around 121 fully-grown, African-savannah bull elephants or 65 double-decker London buses.

It therefore seems reasonable to suggest that if a supposed 'lost' civilization created the Grand Terrace at Baalbek using the same methods of dealing with large weights that we do, the technology they possessed must have been roughly similar to our own at the present time.

It is worth remembering that the mighty Liebherr LTM 11200–9.1 has an operational weight of 96 tonnes and that it carries a counterweight of 202 tonnes. Most of its operational weight is made up of steel – and extremely high-grade steel at that. The processes that go into making such a machine bear testimony to our present level of technical expertise. The mobile crane itself is impressive enough, but the infrastructure necessary to create it speaks of absolute capability in mining, smelting, casting, machining and in our knowledge of chemicals. It tells of our understanding of physics, of our organizational abilities and of our wealth. Such a machine typifies the level to which humanity has come in the 21st century, but it could never be seen as an isolated example because without the complexity of our factories and the cohesion of different aspects of our creative genius, it simply could not exist.

In this one isolated example we see, personified, everything we have become along the long road of development. Bits and pieces of the Liebherr LTM 11200–9.1 undoubtedly come from the four corners of the world and therefore demonstrate the cohesion of a vast series of technological cultures, each co-operating, adept at rapid communication across long distances and all part of a planet that is increasingly learning to pool its resources and pull together.

The ability to create machines such as the Liebherr LTM 11200–9.1 speaks of the consumption of vast amounts of power. Underpinning its reality is capitalism, the very mechanism that has allowed us to become what we are.

At the back of such a system are vast cities, complex global banking institutions and integrated worldwide transportation systems.

Not one of the writers suggesting the existence of pre-existent civilizations – at least none whose work I have read – addresses the implications of what they are proposing. None can say for certain where such a civilization may have been based – because all we can point to are isolated examples of technological genius, spread out around the world. No archaeologist has ever uncovered the remains of anything that looks like a modern 21st-century city, or the footprint of factories capable of producing iron and steel on a massive scale. No remnants of a machine comparable with the Liebherr LTM 11200–9.1 or anything like it have ever been uncovered, either on an archaeological site or accidentally during our own building projects. Everything we see from the distant past is more or less appropriate to its setting, apart from these random examples that simply defy logic.

As I have indicated, technology demands power and that power has to come from somewhere. It is likely that in the future we will find newer and better means of obtaining the power humanity requires, without raping the world of even more of its natural resources. Nuclear power is already a reality and the possibility of nuclear fusion – truly the Eldorado of limitless, cheap power – probably lies not long into the future. Meanwhile we have learned to harness the power of wind and waves, as well as sunlight, though even today these clean alternatives form a relatively tiny part of the power generated in the world.

Getting to an era of nuclear power, and even to the natural alternatives such as power from the Sun, has required many centuries of advancement in science and it is hard to imagine any culture arriving at such possibilities without first having gone through decades or centuries of the utilization of coal and oil. As far as I can ascertain, no trace of vast opencast coal mining from the extremely remote past has ever been found, whereas 'we' have scarred the Earth in such a way that the effects of our efforts would be noticeable tens of thousands of years into the future. To trace the extraction of oil in prehistoric times would be more difficult, but the fact that the reserves we have located in the last century or more were not depleted seems to indicate that much of the Earth's oil had not been exploited in remote antiquity.

If there ever was a fantastic civilization prior to any of the historical ones we know about, where is its footprint? It simply does not exist. Although the natural processes of the Earth mean that land in some part of the planet is either sinking or rising, that continents move about and volcanism gradually eradicates areas, this whole process is an extremely slow one. That some super-civilization once existed in an area of the planet that is now below water is also quite unlikely. Folklore might suggest that there was once a vast island in the middle of the Atlantic, which sank without trace, and many modern writers still search avidly for clues of Atlantis, but geologists state, and with significant evidence on their side, that no such landmass ever existed. Even if Atlantis had been a reality, there is no indication from the ancient stories that it was that much more advanced than other cultures existent at the time. Plato suggests that sailors from Atlantis plied the seas of the world and he also suggests that Atlantis fought wars with other states, but there is nothing in these stories to suggest that the Atlanteans were using jet fighters or inter-continental missiles.

After years of believing that only some pre-existent super-civilization could explain many of the anomalies of the ancient past, I was eventually forced to the conclusion that such a scenario is very, very unlikely. It is inconceivable that all evidence of a society possessed of advanced technology could have disappeared altogether. The historical anomalies do exist, both in concrete terms across the surface of our world, and with regard to knowledge so advanced it rivals our own, but the infrastructure necessary to account for either is totally absent. As with visitors from outer space, I am quite prepared to change my opinions if any hard evidence is forthcoming, but for the moment there simply is none.

Where does that leave us? I have 30 years of research that proves to me that there were at least some people on our planet 5,000 years ago who were as technologically and mathematically adept as we are now – maybe even more so – but if these people were not the remnants of lost super-civilizations or did not come to the Earth in spaceships, where did they come from?

This is a question that has plagued me for years. I knew there was an alternative. My fellow writer Chris Knight and I had even dared to speak about it in the books we had created together, but it took a very long time and a great deal of thought before what seems at first sight an even more unlikely idea than lost civilizations or visiting spacemen began to take on the form of a realistic scenario – and what is more, one that answers all the puzzles.

The only logical conclusion I could draw, and it is one that will immediately make many readers wince, is that the people who created the wonders from prehistory that cannot be explained in any other way most probably came from our own future.

Before I go into the details of the intervention theory of time travel, it is worth looking at the evidence again. Quite apart from major, known civilizations, for example those of the Egyptians and the Babylonians, we have, from the most ancient times, a number of incredibly impressive structures spread around the planet that seem to exist, more or less, in isolation. In other words they do not form part of a cohesive society that can be shown to have regularly used the technical expertise necessary to create such structures. In some cases this inferred expertise is at least equal to our capabilities today. There also exist two fully functioning, integrated measuring systems (which I will explain in due course) based on information regarding the Earth that was not discovered by our own culture until relatively recently, but which was clearly known and used over 5,000 years ago. On the other side of the coin, we have no archaeological or geologically based evidence of any major pre-existent civilization prior to those of which we are aware in the historical record, and neither do we have the merest scrap of concrete proof that our planet was ever visited by philanthropic aliens in the remote past.

Just assuming for a moment that visits from our future could have been made to our past, how would this square with what we find? In fact, it would do so very well. It would explain why no hard evidence of pre-existent cultures has ever been found because such evidence need not exist. Travellers from the future could bring their technology with them, and take it away again afterwards. Their presence would be fleeting and once they were gone there would be no evidence of their having been here, except the structures they had helped to create and the legacy they left behind in terms of helping cultures to advance. Such visitations could easily explain the wealth of mythology and folklore that points to the strange encounters of ancient peoples with 'super-beings', some of which we will analyse later. Such a possibility would also explain the presence of scientific knowledge that no really early culture could possibly have gleaned for itself at such a remote period, and in particular how a measuring system, supposedly not invented until the late 18th century, was fully functioning as early as 3000BC.

At first glance the whole notion may seem absurd, but is it any more far-fetched than alien intervention or the idea of some great antediluvian, highly advanced society which singularly fails to be found in any shape or form? To my way of thinking it is far more likely than either. Once we know the whole story and understand why it was not only fascinating but absolutely essential for our future selves to interfere in the development of the world, and specifically that of humanity, it becomes a whole lot more understandable.

When my mind first began to dwell on such a notion, I came up with all sorts of difficulties associated with the hypothesis, quite aside from the technical problems of actually travelling back in time. I studied everything I could about the feasibility of time travel and discovered that, beyond a few brave souls who were willing to conjecture, nobody really knows whether it could ever be possible or not. Certainly travelling to the past could create significant problems, because almost anything we might do there would undoubtedly have a part to play in what took place henceforth. We might inadvertently change history, and upon travelling back to our own time period we could find things significantly altered. Sooner or later the whole idea would see us running up against paradoxes that would themselves make the whole scenario effectively impossible.

The most famous of these is known as the grandfather paradox. It suggests that if we suddenly took a dislike to our own grandfather, we might choose to travel back in time to a period when Grandfather was himself a child. Having done so, we could take a gun and shoot him dead. But of course we could do no such thing, because if Grandfather never grew up and married, he could not have had children, which means that one of our parents could never have been born and neither could we. This being the case, we would never have existed to go back and murder anyone. It is an unanswerable dilemma and I think it demonstrates beyond doubt that indiscriminate time travel to the past, in which our own free will was the only motivating factor, could never take place. From our perspective the past is fixed – immutable.

All the same, things may not be quite this simple because it is quite possible to build another paradox that absolutely insists that we *do* travel back in time. Supposing I was researching in my local library, looking at old newspapers, and I came across an article that told the story of a young man whose life was saved when he was pushed out of the way of an oncoming train. Upon reading the article I am surprised to discover that the child in question was none other than my grandfather. Imagine my further astonishment when I look at the picture of the person who saved him, because it is without doubt a photograph of me – and what is more the name is the same.

This means that I *must* travel back in time in order to save the life of my grandfather. If I fail to do so he will die as a child, and I will never be born. So, on the one hand, if we travel back in time indiscriminately we may adversely affect our own lives and that of the future in its entirety, but on the other hand if we sometimes fail to do so, our own future and that of our world might still be adversely affected. As unlikely as my second example might be, looked at this way, what would be required is some sort of model in which 'essential' travel in time was possible, but in which the consequences of indiscriminate interference could never be an issue.

I spent more than a few years thinking about the supposed paradoxes of time travel. I asked myself – 'If humanity ever does travel into the past, why are we not aware of such travellers visiting our own timeframe?' It seemed that every possible model I built was deficient in some respect. And then, as is so often the case, when I had put the matter on one side and got on with other things, the answers came to me. It arrived by way of a dream and suddenly I could not understand why it had all puzzled me so much.

CHAPTER THREE

Intervention Theory

I found myself walking down a long, straight corridor that seemed to go on to infinity. As I walked I could see innumerable doors leading off the corridor to the right and to the left. Each door had a large handle and a small aperture at its centre, like the ones on pictures of cell doors in prisons. I stopped to look through the spy hole of one or two. What I saw surprised me, even in a dream. It appeared that there were individual scenes taking place beyond the doors. As I peered through different doors, all manner of tableaux unfolded before my eyes. It all looked perfectly normal and modern as I spied through the doors closest to me, but as I walked on down the corridor, so the pictures displayed to me took on a more and more historical feel.

Several doors on, the view displayed to me through a particular aperture was one of a dark and brooding city, with tall chimneys belching out smoke onto a generally gloomy landscape. Only one door further on I could see the bright, clear vista of a summer cornfield, with labourers toiling away patiently beneath a benevolent sky. Further on still, I looked through an aperture that displayed a scene of the most unimaginable horror. Uniformed men crouched in deep mud as shells and bullets passed overhead. There were human bodies and, worse still, parts of bodies to be seen everywhere. I knew instinctively that what I was looking at must be the First World War or some other 20th-century conflict in which the greatest battle was merely to stay alive. From the very start I had tried to turn the large brass handle on every door I passed, only to find that all the doors were firmly locked. I could see what was happening behind them, but it was impossible to gain entry to any one of these alternative worlds.

The further I walked, the older the scenes became. Through one door was a vista onto a frozen river, with muffled peasants dragging bundles of wood towards a multi-towered town. Through another was what looked like a Victorian street scene, with innumerable horse carriages and vans; shops with produce spilling out onto the pavement and children bowling hoops and skipping on the cobbled street. One by one I tried all the handles and looked through the spy holes at a world that was growing more distant in time with each door as I walked on down the corridor. To someone such as me who is fascinated by history it was very frustrating. I longed to walk through into some of these scenes and to take my place amidst something so different and informative, but every door remained barred to me. I could see all these events in absolute clarity, and could even hear what was taking place, but I could not be part of any of it.

Only after I had walked a great distance and tried to enter a hundred or more doors did I find something entirely different. There, ahead of me on the left was a door that was standing wide open. I approached and gingerly looked around the edge of the open door. What I saw was a large, oak-panelled room, replete with dark, heavy furniture, hanging tapestries and portraits. Above was an ornate, hammer-beam ceiling and on the floor there were rushes and dried wild flowers.

There were many people in the chamber, both men and women. All wore period Elizabethan costume and were talking animatedly, one to another. Taking my opportunity I stepped through the doorway and immediately found that I was in the midst of this gathering. I looked down at myself and realized that suddenly I was wearing the same apparel as everyone in the room. Nobody stared at me and in fact the smiles and nods I registered seemed to indicate that I was no stranger in this gathering. One or two of the women present even dropped a slight curtsy as I came upon them.

Further into the room was the sound of music and I could see dancing taking place. To my left was a large table, filled with cooked meats, pastries and fruit. Some of the seats around the table were occupied by people resting or eating and at one end of the table was a very high-backed oak chair. The seat was ornately carved and padded, but nobody occupied it.

Now I found myself standing by this seat and for some reason I was not in the least surprised to see my own name, Alan Butler, carved in relief at the top of the chair back and picked out in gold leaf. It seemed to be proof to me that there was a place for me within this gathering, and that in no way was I out of time or an alien interloper.

Moments later I awoke, and through the following day, as different parts of the dream came back to me, I began to piece together its meaning; I came to understand that by way of the dream my subconscious mind had created a perfect metaphor for what I would come to call intervention theory.

It is quite natural for us to think about time as being a linear phenomenon. We are born, we grow through childhood to be adults and after our allotted span we die. We accept this state of affairs and indeed, prior to the modern industrial age, the linear nature of time was even more apparent. Most people lived on the land. Year by year they followed the cycles of the season, from planting to harvest, from summer to winter – an irrevocable clock, the hands of which turned alongside the Earth on its yearly journey around the Sun.

The linear nature of time is reflected in the most routine aspects of the physical world, for example cause and effect. I stand on the mound and make a pitch. The hitter strikes the ball and a home run is the result. Poets have described time as being an 'arrow' or a 'winged chariot', always emphasizing the fact that it travels in one direction only and that once an event has taken place, it cannot be altered in any way.

Just as in my dream, even if we could travel back down the corridor of time and perhaps view its events, how could we possibly gain entry to it? As with the grandfather paradox, logic asserts that even the slightest alteration in events with regard to a past that has already happened could have catastrophic consequences on the future. This is why some scientists commenting on time travel to the past, for example Professor Stephen Hawking, have envisaged some sort of agency or immutable law (often jokingly referred to as the time police) that would prevent incursions into the past.

However, in my dream, not all the doors on the past were barred to me. I found one door that was wide open. Nobody in that timeframe was surprised to see me, and my name carved into a chair indicated that there was nothing unusual about my being there. But why should entry to this timeframe be allowed, when every other door was barred to me?

As strange as it sounds, perhaps the reason I was allowed to travel back to the Elizabethan scene was because I genuinely had been there. If this doesn't quite make sense let us pretend that my dream was a real experience and then think of it from the point of view of someone else in the same Tudor room. Someone who is living a perfectly ordinary life back in Elizabethan England receives an invitation to a banquet and dance. The person in question arrives on the due date and whilst they are enjoying themselves they see or are introduced to me. To them the encounter is the most natural thing in the world. If I make a good impression the person will remember me once the banquet is over – I will have become a part of their time frame.

From that point on, right through the 16th and subsequent centuries, my presence at the gathering will be a part of history, even though I have not yet been born. And then, on some specific date in the 21st century, I take a trip back in time and fulfil the requirements by being at the Tudor function. I can make the journey because I *was* there, and so the door to the timeframe in question is open to me.

Whilst I am in the historical time frame I cannot do or say anything that I *did not* do or say, but in a way this is irrelevant. My words and actions were already written into history before I embarked, so even though it appears to me whilst I am at the banquet that I am exercising my own free will, whatever I do or say will become part of that time frame – it will already be history.

This whole scenario might seem utterly counterintuitive, but that does not necessarily mean it is wrong. It is equally counterintuitive to envisage the same particle existing simultaneously in two totally different places, but in the strange world of quantum physics it happens all the time. Following the dictates of what is known as 'superposition', extremely small particles such as atoms or electrons can indeed frequent two or in fact infinite locations at the same time. This is so illogical that many scientists prefer not to overheat their brains by thinking about it – but it happens, nevertheless.

What I am suggesting does not contradict the linear nature of time – it merely places another possibility onto it. This possibility is the existence of 'time loops' which would allow one to travel back in time, but only if the visit we intend to make already exists in history. We might *try* to embark on a journey to any part of the past, but if we were genuinely never there, we will most probably remain where we were in the first place, no matter what mechanism we use to take our journey.

Under intervention theory it isn't that there is any external force, such as the time police, making sure we do not interfere in the past in a way that will have a bearing on the future. It's a little like setting off on a protracted journey from Europe to Australia, without one's passport. It doesn't matter how much we beg and plead in the arrivals lounge of our intended airport, we will not be allowed to enter the country without the relevant documents. This fact does not necessarily prevent us from embarking, but we can't meet, talk to, or interact with anyone beyond the airport arrivals – the door to Australia will be closed to us.

Of course I am certainly not the first person to muse on such matters and so I began a concerted search to see how this particular hypothetical view of time travel might square with the ideas and knowledge of those whose business it is to peer into the furthest recesses of physics.

The closest I came to my model for travel into the past was in the work of Igor Novikov, a Russian theoretical astrophysicist and cosmologist. Born in 1935, Novikov was the head of the department of Relativistic Astrophysics at the Russian Space Research Institute in Moscow between 1974 and 1990. Subsequently he held down a series of other important positions and was a professor at Moscow State University.

During the 1980s Professor Novikov put forward what is known as 'the Novikov self-consistency principle'. Put at it simplest this suggests that regarding a time travel event that would give rise to a paradox, or indeed to any change to the past at all, the probability of such an event would be zero.

Novikov's suggestion is born out of 'closed time-like curves'. These were first postulated in 1937 by Willem van Stockum, a Dutch mathematician. Van Stockum was interested in the field equations of the theory of general relativity. He showed mathematically that in a closed time-like curve, the world-line of an object through space–time follows a curious path, which eventually ends at the exact coordinates in space and time from where it started. Van Stockum died tragically during the Second World War and his ideas were taken up and elaborated in 1949 by another mathematician, the Austrian Kurt Gödel.

The suggestion that closed time-like curves can exist is dependent on the fact that extreme gravity can curve space–time in a way that may allow time to loop back on itself. As a rule, those commenting on the possibility of time travel by way of closed time-like curves suggest that the mechanisms utilized to make such journeys could involve black holes or wormholes in space.

Such ideas as closed time-like curves were revolutionary because they showed that one need not contradict the known laws of physics in order to travel back in time. This was the point at which the notion of 'paradoxes' began to develop. Novikov was well aware of the problem and it was with such paradoxes in mind that he was eventually able to put forward his self-consistency principle.

Novikov suggests, and many physicists agree with him, that it is quite possible to take a journey to the past, utilizing closed time-like curves. However, once arriving at a particular destination in history, although it will be possible to *affect* history, it would be quite impossible to alter it in any way – the mathematics inherent in general relativity simply do not allow for it because the probability that such a history-changing event could ever take place is zero.

I turned my brain inside out in order to understand the implications of what Novikov and a wealth of physicists since were saying, and I could not envisage any part of my own intervention theory that was at odds with Novikov's principle. If one was to travel to the past in the way I suggest, as far as I can see no paradox takes place, neither is one attempting to *alter* history in any way. On the contrary, by choosing to make such a journey one is simply *confirming* what (in the future) will be a genuine part of history.

In order to make such a journey one would utilize the 'time-like loop' that Willem van Stockum and many physicists subsequently have suggested. Returning *from* the past would be just as technologically mind-blowing as going back in time, but not so philosophically puzzling. Travelling forward in time is quite possible. This is because of a phenomenon known as time dilation. Time is related to space and it is a fact that the faster one travels, relative to one's point of embarkation, the faster time will pass for anyone left behind and the slower it will pass for whoever is with you on the journey. So if you set off on a circular journey into space, achieving a great speed, whilst you and your passengers experience only a few days or weeks of time passing aboard your spacecraft, months, years or centuries could be passing on the Earth. It sounds weird but it is certainly true.

I do not suggest, and neither did Novikov, that to undertake any journey into the past would be a simple matter. Some physicists think that the amount of sheer energy needed to undertake such a trip would be greater than we could ever harness. There could be innumerable difficulties but, on the other hand, as a species we have proved our ingenuity on countless occasions in the past and surely the same will be true with regard to time travel. I do not doubt for a moment that if we survive long enough as a species, and if time travel into the past is indeed possible, one day we will achieve it. In fact, if intervention theory is true then we 'must' travel in time and will probably do so quite routinely.

For the moment, time travel into the past is purely theoretical but I would argue that we have ample evidence to suggest that it has taken place and that it is most likely taking place right now. It appears to me that the historical record of the Earth is replete with examples of intervention. The remainder of this book itemizes many of them, and also explains why intervention has been necessary and even vital to our development, as well as to the very existence of life on our planet.

I know from long discussions with colleagues about intervention that it raises great puzzles in the minds of many people, because intervention *seems* to be responsible for paradoxes of its own. As I mentioned earlier, we live in a world of cause and effect. The idea of looping back in time to fulfil a historical happening seems to blur the concept of cause and effect.

For example, let us suggest that one day I am walking on a foggy hillside in a mountainous region when I come to a sign that says 'Dangerous Cliff Ahead'. I cannot see the sudden disappearance of the path because of the fog and without the sign I would almost certainly have plunged to my death, but I turn back and am safe. Many years later I have the opportunity to travel back in time. I take with me a signboard exactly like the one I encountered in the past, and place it in front of the precipitous drop. I have undertaken this exercise some weeks or months before being alerted by the signboard and so I have probably saved my own life.

Some people are made uneasy by such a story, partly because of the notion of cause and effect. I suspect that the mental confusion arises because in this instance the idea to place the signboard in that dangerous location came after the event in which my life was saved. In other words, the effect appeared in the timeline before the cause. However, I think we have to constantly look at the situation from the point of the advancing timeline at any given moment. My life was saved by seeing the sign. It does not matter a jot *where* the sign came from or *who* put it where it is. Such a consideration is outside my frame of reference as the hill-walker. As far as I am aware it could have been a local authority that authorized the placement of the warning sign, or some thoughtful fellow rambler. All that matters is that I reacted to the warning.

Later, when I have the means to travel in time, I am able to go to the site and place the sign – ahead of my arrival as the walker. I do so as a result of a conscious decision and am able to do so because this is what actually happened. I am sure Professor Novikov would approve and I cannot personally see how there is any paradox. True, it might be odd, but then the universe is a very odd place.

Friends and colleagues have often asked me: 'If people are constantly travelling from the future to the past, why are we not aware of the fact? Why are we not being told by the visitors themselves that this is the case?'

From a purely practical point of view there might be all manner of reasons why visitors from the future, who may be in our midst at any time, do not choose to tell us where they come from. It could be a common, well-thought-out decision, made at some stage in the future as a strategy to avoid polluting the timeline. However, such considerations are actually immaterial. According to Novikov's self-consistency principle, we cannot do anything in the past that was not done – in other words we cannot alter history in any way. Therefore, if no traveller from the future has so far divulged their point of origin, they cannot do so. This is a state of affairs that may change at any moment, but if it has not happened so far, it 'cannot' happen prior to today.

It took a very long time for me to truly understand the implications of intervention. In the end I was content to look at the evidence. If there is anything in the mechanism I did not or do not understand, I remain content to learn more at some stage in the future. After all, I can travel on any morning from my home in the north of England to London, in order to attend a publishing meeting, but it is not necessary for me to understand how the locomotive that pulls the train works, or to comprehend the complexity of the system of signals that allows my train to get there safely.

What really matters is the change in one's world-view that takes place once intervention is accepted as a possibility. Its existence answers so many questions, deals with a multitude of historical puzzles and makes sense of much of my research that was so confusing before. So, if only for the sake of the exercise, allow me to lead you on a new and different journey through the history of the Earth and us, its inhabitants. Such a journey might fascinate and illuminate you as much as it has me.

CHAPTER FOUR

The Building Blocks of Life

I want to start with one of the most important interventions that I believe took place by humanity from our future into our past, though it was not the first. The very first intervention happened right back around the time the Earth was an infant and I intend to deal with that later in the book. In the meantime my starting point comes 3.4 billion years ago, which is around 1 billion years after the Earth came into being.

It was around this time that something quite remarkable took place on what at the time would have been a most inhospitable world as far as we are concerned. It was the dawn of life. There are many suggestions as to exactly *how* something as incredibly unlikely as life first began, but it has to be said from the outset that life's emergence is still shrouded in mystery.

What we do know is that in the long period between 3.4 billion years ago and now, in the part of the world that would eventually become Australia, layers of once living creatures became fixed as fossils in sedimentary rock, where researchers find them today. These stromatolites, as they are called, were once colonies of cyanobacteria, a primitive life form otherwise known as blue-green algae. Cyanobacteria served, and still serve, a very important function as far as we are concerned because they are tiny oxygen factories. And far from existing only as fossils, cyanobacteria of an identical sort to those that created the stromatolites are still to be found alive and well in Australia.

Many scientists think that it was the existence of blue-green algae that, across many millions of years, made the Earth habitable to the more complex, oxygen-dependent life forms that came much later. They still serve their essential function and have remained generally unchanged, proving that when evolution gets something very right, it doesn't need to alter much, no matter how much time passes.

As useful as the finding of stromatolites proved to be, it still creates problems because even a single cyanobacteria is a remarkable piece of biological engineering that contains DNA, which is an incredibly complex structure that exists inside every life form across our planet. Without DNA there could be no life at all but the first living creatures we can recognize from this truly ancient period already possessed it.

What is DNA?

DNA, which stands for deoxyribonucleic acid is a molecule (a molecule is a chemical substance that is formed when different atoms bond together). A good example of a fairly simple molecule is water, which contains two atoms of hydrogen for every one atom of oxygen. Molecules can be very simple or extremely complex. These days humanity is capable of producing long-chain molecules that do not exist naturally, for example in the creation of plastics, but nature has done a pretty good job on its own when it comes to long molecules, and DNA is a prime example.

DNA is truly remarkable, even if the chemicals it contains are fairly simple. It looks, as most people are aware these days, like a double helix with the appearance of a spiral ladder, and each section or rung of the ladder represents a pair of what are known as nucleotides. The nucleotides themselves are molecules and are made up of three components – in each case these are the sides of the ladder and half of each rung. In DNA the rungs of the ladder are split in two and are only held together by hydrogen bonds. When the DNA replicates, it splits down the middle of these rungs and each half of the ladder becomes the basis of a new ladder. The rungs of the ladder are made up of chemical bases. The bases are in fixed pairs but they can appear on the ladder of DNA in any sequence, and this is the way messages are written within the DNA that passes on the information it carries. Amongst these are instructions for its own replication and the job it undertakes informing living cells how they should behave and what they should become. A single set of instructions is called a 'gene' and as living creatures we inherit half our genes from our mother and half from our father.

Reading the Genome

DNA itself is not all that complicated. What makes it so stunning is that so much information is carried by the DNA strand. At the start of the present millennium scientists achieved something magnificent. They were able to read the DNA sequence, or genome, of human beings. Each gene has four nucleotides, the names of which are shortened for convenience into letters. The letters are A for adenine, T for thymine, C for cytosine and G for guanine. And although there are only these four letters to deal with, they appear so many times in the human genome that it contains around 3,000,000,000 letters!

Most current theories suggest that the DNA molecule is a spontaneous creation of nature, though even many scientists remain baffled as to how something so absolutely complex could have come about by chance.

Way back in the late 1920s, some time before DNA was discovered, it was believed that life may have developed spontaneously from the cocktail of chemicals that existed in the Earth's early oceans. It was suggested at this time that these chemicals, acted upon by the Sun's rays and by electrical storms, produced what was known as a thin primordial soup within Earth's oceans. This contained organic molecules. The idea was that this thin soup thickened over time and that what resulted were amino acids – the chemicals that are essential to life. Experiments were carried out in laboratories in which the necessary chemicals and electrical charges were present, and these showed that the idea of primordial soup was a possibility; but although the amino acids did in fact result from the experiments, life did not generate spontaneously. In other words, it is one thing to have all the chemicals to hand to found life, but something quite different to make them live.

Even though the DNA of the first living creatures on the Earth was far less complicated than that of many modern living species, it still represented a biochemical miracle. Author Lyall Watson, in his book *Supernature* considered that the chances against the DNA molecule coming together on its own, spontaneously, is greater than the number of atoms in the known universe. All of the information necessary to create a human being – or an elephant or a blue whale for that matter – exists in every strand of DNA contained in that creature. In human beings the strand itself is about 2.2 metres in length and this exists in virtually every cell of our bodies. Nature has an ingenious way of packaging DNA inside cells, the largest of which are absolutely tiny, and the whole is a genuine miracle of biological engineering.

In order to see the average cell it has to be magnified 1,000 times. If this was its actual size, the DNA strand within it would measure around 3 kilometres when untwisted. It is possible to work out roughly how far the DNA in an average human being would stretch and the result is incredible. Absolute measurements are not possible but in the body of a human there may be 10 trillion to 50 trillion cells containing DNA and the length of the strands in each is around 2 metres. Whichever figure is correct means that the total length of DNA present in every human being would be enough to stretch to the Moon and back many hundreds or even thousands of times.

One of the most amazing things about human DNA is that much of it is thought to be junk. During the long road of evolution that led from those first single-celled creatures to us, a multitude of different species have come and gone – not only animals but plants, too. The stages of evolution between cyanobacteria and human beings were complicated, with many different species and a fair few evolutionary dead-ends. Every plant, animal or whatever, on the evolutionary journey, had components of DNA necessary to its form, shape and characteristics that are not relevant to us. It is a little like taking a tremendously long journey down a winding lane. Every memory of that journey is encapsulated in each strand of our DNA but only the sights and sounds around us right now are truly important to what we are at this stage of our evolution. All the same, we are far from fully understanding DNA and it is quite possible that parts of this so-called junk DNA are of critical importance.

The real problem with DNA is that there is nothing in the fossil record before the stromatolites to indicate how it came about. As far as can be ascertained, it is as if DNA didn't exist – and then suddenly it did, with all its components. This has led some scientists to suggest that DNA may have come to the Earth as a passenger on a meteorite, or more likely a comet, but in order to accept such a possibility we would also have to accept that life of a similar sort to that on Earth exists elsewhere. Bearing in mind the sheer number of stars, even in our own local galaxy, this is a pretty safe bet. But the possibility of such life being present on a comet (an accumulation of dust and ice) and then surviving the unbelievable variations in temperature that comets undergo as they circle our own sun is surely very low. After this the DNA would have to somehow enter the Earth's atmosphere, with all the dangers such a journey implies to any fragile substance. It's a very long shot, but is probably statistically slightly more likely than DNA having suddenly appeared by accident.

To those of a religious persuasion DNA is not a problem, and some creationists use it as possible proof for the existence of God. After all, DNA is so amazing and so very unlikely that one might easily ascribe it to the intervention of a deity. Unfortunately, such a suggestion does little to convince those of a scientific bent. The very existence of God is a matter of faith and it cannot be proven scientifically. Therefore, the scientist might say, if we cannot prove the existence of God, we certainly cannot ascribe to him the creation of the DNA molecule.

I have an alternative explanation for the sudden arrival of DNA upon the Earth. We know from the experiments carried out as early as the late 1920s and repeated so many times since, that the primordial oceans of the Earth were a perfect receptor for early life. Even a relatively small amount of cyanobacteria introduced into the primordial oceans would have proliferated and spread quickly across the planet. And if the Earth was eventually going to become the incubator for much more complex forms of life, this was absolutely necessary.

At the time life first appeared, the Earth's atmosphere was a cauldron of noxious gases. The land that did exist was unstable and subject to constant volcanic activity. The Earth was also being regularly bombarded with meteorites – debris left over from the formation of the solar system. Neither human beings, nor indeed any of the advanced life forms that inhabit our planet today could have survived for even a few minutes in such an environment. One of the most common gases in Earth's atmosphere at the time was carbon dioxide, which spells a very quick death to oxygen-dependent creatures such as us.

This is not the case for the humble cyanobacteria, which relishes a carbon-dioxide-laden environment. There are forms of cyanobacteria that can survive in the harshest of conditions. Many are nitrogen-fixing and all serve the incredibly valuable function of 'locking up' carbon.

A large percentage of the Earth's rocks are composed of limestone. This is a sedimentary rock and it has been used by humanity for thousands of years to build some of its most impressive structures. Surprisingly, it wasn't until the 1950s that scientists finally discovered how limestone had been made. It had been known for a long time that fossils were regularly found in limestone, and these were always those of primitive sea-dwellers, but many examples of limestone are extremely fine-grained and do not contain apparent fossils.

Limestone is a sedimentary rock, some of which is composed of fine-grained silt, of the sort that is deposited by rivers into the marine environment. This accumulated sediment becomes what is known as 'lime mud' the precursor of limestone. It is only when the pressures increase, by more sediment and debris accumulating above the mud over millions of years, that limestone is produced. But it turned out that sediment supplied by rivers is not the main component of limestone. Examinations of lime mud from shallow seas in the Caribbean showed that by far the largest amount of the mud is made up of incredibly small needle-shaped crystals of a mineral known as aragonite. This is a form of calcite and originates in the bodies of cyanobacteria; when the cyanobacteria dies, these tiny crystals sink to the seabed and gradually accumulate until lime mud is formed, and ultimately limestone.

For millions upon millions of years the cyanobacteria and related organisms formed huge blooms on the Earth's oceans. Using a form of photosynthesis, cyanobacteria utilizes sunlight to break down carbon dioxide into organic compounds. These are used to create the bodies of the cyanobacteria and they also allow it to multiply. However, some of the carbon in the process becomes locked into cyanobacteria itself, and this in turn forms the aragonite that sinks to the seabed when the cyanobacteria dies. The result, across billions of years, was that a significant part of the carbon that had once existed in Earth's atmosphere became 'locked' into limestone – an estimated 65–100 quadrillion tonnes!

Slowly but surely this opened up the way for more complex life forms to evolve. As the level of oxygen in the atmosphere increased, all of which was created by the cyanobacteria and their relatives the plants, some newly evolving species began to breathe the oxygen and to exhale carbon dioxide.

It was a very, very long journey but it was made possible by the fact that so much carbon was being locked away into the Earth itself, and was kept out of the atmosphere. What is more, the cyanobacteria and their relatives were increasing the amount of oxygen, which is a by-product of their own lifecycle. Evolution made certain that new niches, created by the way the cyanobacteria was changing the world, were exploited by newer and more complex forms of life.

This is a truly amazing story, but the most remarkable thing about it is how the DNA necessary to establish the first cyanobacteria and other primitive forms of life came to exist in the first place. However, when one accepts the basic principles of intervention theory, the answer is obvious. The first forms of life, complete with their primitive but essential DNA, were present in Earth's early oceans because humanity put them there.

Many forms of cyanobacteria have hardly changed at all, and we know the ones that created those first stromatolites are still alive, well and living in Australia. Even a relatively small amount of these tiny creatures, taken back around 3.4 billion years and placed into an environment that would be like Christmas to them, would have proliferated rapidly. In all probability, at this stage of our planet, nothing else would have been necessary. The driving machine of evolution would have taken care of everything that followed.

As with so much else in the intervention theory, it is simply irrelevant to ask the question – 'But where did DNA come from in the first place?' The only reason we ask this question is because we retain the view that time must 'always' be linear – that it has to run from A to Z and that under no circumstance can it be 'circular' in nature. The truth is that the cyanobacteria were where they needed to be at the right time. Since we have an unlimited supply of this life form still living happily in our planet's oceans, the puzzle of where it came from is no puzzle at all.

Once again it is necessary to look at the sequence of events from the perspective of the developing planet. Some 3.4 billion years ago, the oceans of the Earth were a rich soup of chemicals, brought up from the centre of the cooling but still highly volcanic Earth and deposited in the oceans. Sunlight shining down on this 'broth', together with the tremendous electrical activity of almost constant storms, acted upon the oceans until they offered exactly the right sort of environment for cyanobacteria. It was at this point that cyanobacteria were taken from our future and deposited in the primordial oceans. In other words, they were present when they were needed.

If this theory is correct, no matter how hard scientists look for the precursors of DNA, they will never find them.

These earliest specks of life were just as subject to the processes of natural selection as anything that followed them. In some places they remained more or less the same as they had always been, right up until today, but in other environments they had to adapt to different pressures and circumstances. What resulted were gradually more complex forms of life, which were themselves subject to natural selection – and so on, right up to the diversity of species we see in our world today.

CHAPTER FIVE

Monkey or Man?

eginning in December 1912 and continuing right up until 1952, one
of the greatest hoaxes ever to have been perpetrated on the scientific
community took place in Great Britain. It all started when Charles
Dawson (1864–1916), a well respected amateur archaeologist, presented parts
of a human-looking skull to a meeting of the Geological Society of London
on 18 December 1912. Dawson claimed that the skull fragments had been
found by workmen at a gravel pit in Piltdown, East Sussex, England. Some of
those present at the meeting showed a definite and immediate interest in what
Dawson showed them, because the fragments of bone had all the hallmarks
of being from a very special human being.

One of the members of the geological society, Arthur Smith Woodward,
who was also keeper of geology at the British Museum, returned to the site
with Dawson and there they found further parts of the skull and half the
jawbone. The world of science was delighted because many people at the
time believed that what Dawson had discovered was nothing less than the
'missing link' – in other words the skull of a near human that bridged the
gap between ape and man.

Almost immediately there were some experts who thought that the whole
'Piltdown Man' incident had been a carefully prepared hoax and indeed, in
the fullness of time, this turned out to be the truth. Although some experts
continued to believe in the veracity of the find, right up until 1952, even the

most diehard supporter of the remains had, in the end, to admit that what Dawson had actually presented to the Geological Society was the skull of a modern human being and the carefully doctored jawbone of an orang-utan.

Science does not like to be left with egg on its face and the repercussions of the Piltdown Man incident remain with us in some respects – not least of all in terms of just how sensitive palaeontology is when it comes to remains that might link humanity with its ape past. The whole situation is made slightly more complicated because by no means everyone in the world believes that human beings did evolve from an ape-like common ancestor. Creationists, in particular, are adamant (despite all the evidence to the contrary) that humanity was made directly by God, as is indicated in the Old Testament of the Bible. Although few, if any, of those involved in the study of evolution have any truck whatsoever with Creation as a concept, there remains a certain 'sensitivity' regarding anything to do with humanity and its ape-like grandparents.

One of the results of all of this is that experts in the field now make it plain, at every opportunity, that there is *no* missing link between apes and humans and that all the evolutionary stages of our journey from ape to human are now adequately represented by fossil evidence. I am not the only interested individual to doubt this claim somewhat, and in order to explain why, it will be necessary to look at the situation as it appears at this time.

Generally speaking it is now an accepted fact that human beings come at the end of a long road, leading from those very first single-celled creatures that inhabited the early oceans of the world. Over millions of years, species had to adapt in order to survive and flourish. There was no thought process involved and, as was first suggested by Charles Darwin (1809–82), what took place was a case of the survival of the fittest. When any living thing reproduces, especially over long periods of time, there will always be occasions when mistakes are made in the copying of the DNA. These can lead to alterations in the creature concerned. In the case of mammals an animal might end up with a longer tail, a more pointed snout or stronger musculature than is the case with its peers. Mostly, these mistakes in the copying of the DNA come to nothing.

At worst, the adaptation will make life more difficult for the animal concerned and as a result will prevent it from breeding successfully or frequently. On the other hand, there are sometimes genetic alterations that turn out to be distinctly advantageous. These might allow a creature to run faster and therefore hunt more easily, to have better camouflage and thereby avoid predation or to simply be better at adapting to changing circumstances. Such an animal will be more successful in its environment and its breeding rate will be better. As a result the genetic changes that were originally an accident will be carried on to the next generation, which in turn will pass them onto its own offspring and so on.

Little by little this can lead not simply to changes in the species concerned but to entirely new species. The process is ultimately led by alterations in environment, by increased competition for food, and by possible diversity in food opportunities. It is seen at every level throughout evolution. In the case of animals, predators may become swifter, more powerful and more cunning. Prey species, if they are to survive at all, must adapt too. They might themselves become much faster, so they can escape the predator, or, like elephants and the rhinoceros, become so large and fearsome that predators tend to leave them alone.

So it has continued for all forms of life. Some plants became spiny or poisonous, a number of insects developed chemical defences; snakes ultimately came to possess venom, for defence and to kill their prey. Meanwhile, not all forms of life could adapt quickly enough, especially to catastrophes, and as a result they failed to breed at all and became extinct. In other cases the changes were eventually dramatic, as for example the massive whales which, like us, ultimately evolved from small shrew-like creatures.

After the two eras of the great reptiles, during what are known as the Jurassic and the Cretaceous periods, our own distant ancestors began to predominate in some areas of the Earth. These were mammals – creatures that were warm-blooded, which no longer laid eggs and which suckled their young. The earliest mammals extend back around 200 million years, but these were tiny creatures. It was not until around 130 million years ago that marsupial-like mammals began to appear, and only 65 million years ago that the first primates began to develop. It is from this very recent group of animals that modern apes and also modern human beings eventually evolved.

Modern human beings have existed for the last 160,000–200,000 years or so. We know that this is the case because fossils of human beings who were identical to us have been found, dating back to this period. The oldest ever examples of bones from modern humans were found in Ethiopia by a team from the University of California headed by palaeontologist Tim White. Meanwhile, there are so many examples of fossils of hominids that predate human beings, but which are thought to be our ancestors, that the whole situation is bewildering.

The greater and lesser apes split apart and became distinct species around 18 million years ago. Then somewhat later, around 14 million years ago, the hominid species that would eventually lead to humanity, parted company with the great apes and began the long journey that would lead to *Homo sapiens*.

The oldest fossils of creatures that most likely existed on the path from ape-like hominids to human beings are the australopithecines that existed around 4 million years ago. The creatures themselves were bipedal, and in terms of their teeth they were quite similar to human beings. However, their brain size was much closer to that of an ape than a modern human.

Various examples of *Australopithecus* fossils have been found and it is believed that the genus evolved in eastern Africa and that it eventually spread all over the continent. It was once thought that the species became extinct around 2 million years ago but examples of *Australopithecus boisei* have been found that approach 1 million years of age. Most of the examples found indicate that early *Australopithecus* was no more than about 1.5 metres in height, with males significantly larger than females, probably by up to 50 per cent. As a genus *Australopithecus* most likely ate fruit, nuts and root plants;

indispensible as it may be on the road from ape to man, the creature did not bear any striking similarity to modern humans and had an appearance much more like an ape. The brain of *Australopithecus* was only around 30 per cent of that of modern humans.

The first example of this genus was discovered in the 1920s and further specimens have been unearthed repeatedly between then and now. There seems no doubt that this was a successful group and it is also clear that as time passed, slightly different forms of *Australopithecus* began to appear. There is now a bewildering array of australopithecines of various sorts, one of the most important of which seems to be *Australopithecus boisei*. A cranium from this creature was found in 1959 by Mary Leakey, whose family have been crucial in the finding of early human-ancestor fossils. What sets *Australopithecus boisei* apart from earlier examples of the genus are its more vertically set face, alterations in the layout and size of its teeth, and a larger cranial capacity and therefore a bigger brain.

None of these creatures are classified under the genus *Homo*, which of course is our own genus. The first creature to have that distinction is an *Australopithecus*-derived character known as *Homo habilis*. The first example of *H. habilis* was also found by the Leakey team, in 1960 in the Olduvai Gorge of Tanzania. What sets *H. habilis* apart from his earlier ancestors is, once again, an increased cranial size, but also evidence, from the bones of the hand, of a precision grip. This grip is especially important because it suggests that *H. habilis* was a tool-maker – which surely has to be a milestone on the road from ape-like ancestor to man. *H. habilis* had a flatter face than his older ancestors, though he had longer and more ape-like arms than some of his other cousins. Probably most important of all, it is accepted by at least some experts that *Homo habilis* gave way, through evolution, to *Homo ergaster*, a creature that itself is thought to occupy an important position on the way to modern human beings.

Looking at the skull of *H. ergaster* one can easily see why. Once again the face is much flatter than that of an ape; the cranium approaches that of a human and the brain size is much larger than that of the australopithecines. An almost complete skeleton of this creature was found in Kenya in 1984 and this offers us a good view of *H. ergaster*'s size and general characteristics. *Homo ergaster* may well have been capable of rudimentary speech and the tools he made were more advanced than those of any of his predecessors. Males were still significantly larger than females, but it is obvious that sexual dimorphism by this stage was starting to approach that of modern humans, and was much less emphasized than in the case of *Australopithecus*.

As things stand there is now only one more step on the way to modern man. This comes in the form of a creature known as *Homo heidelbergensis*. This ape-man was very similar to *H. ergaster*, but had a larger brain – in fact not too much different than that of modern humans. Also *H. heidelbergensis* was tall, probably as much as 1.8 metres in height; it was most likely a hunter of large game and could probably speak. There is some disagreement as to whether this is a direct ancestor of our closely associated cousin, Neanderthal man, or whether it represents a different species. *Homo heidelbergensis* probably became extinct as recently as around 400,000 years ago.

A side issue is provided by yet another hominid, this one known as *Homo erectus*. There is great argument as to whether *H. erectus* is merely a different form of *H. ergaster*, which would make it an extremely close relative of ours, or whether it is a divergent species that developed in Asia. *Homo erectus* is found as far east as China. It is likely that *H. erectus* lived in hunter-gatherer communities – he certainly used tools and created weapons for hunting – but all things considered, does not appear to be quite as advanced as *H. heidelbergensis* and had a smaller cranial capacity.

All of which brings us finally to the last two remaining representatives of the *Homo* genus. These are *Homo neanderthalensis* and *Homo sapiens* (us).

Probably the most intriguing member of the hominid family, apart from our own, is that of Neanderthal man. It is still uncertain whether this hominid was a subspecies of modern humans or if it was a totally different species. The first example of bones related to Neanderthal man was discovered in the

Neander Valley in Germany in 1856. Since that time many examples have been found, and across a wide area. It is likely that Neanderthals developed from yet another hominid, this one known as *Homo rhodesiensis* who was also one of our own ancestors. True Neanderthal man most likely appeared around 200,000 years ago (though opinions differ). The Neanderthals were quite successful and remains have been found in most of Europe south of the Balkans, including southern Britain, but Neanderthals also lived as far east as the Ukraine and extending down into the Middle East – where significant evidence has been found in and around Israel.

What sets Neanderthal man apart from modern man are some of his skeletal characteristics. He was slightly shorter in height, much more robust in build and far stronger than modern man. Neanderthal skulls have more pronounced brow ridges, though their cranial capacity is at least as large as our own and maybe greater. Neanderthals lived in communities, were hunters and gatherers, made quite sophisticated tools and may even have had a form of religion because it is suggested they buried their dead with some ceremony.

Genetic studies have shown that between 1 and 4 per cent of our own genetic makeup is Neanderthal, indicating that at some stage in the past there was a genetic connection (possibly interbreeding) between Neanderthals and *Homo sapiens*. There is little direct evidence that the disappearance of the Neanderthals, probably around 24,000 years ago, was as a result of fighting between them and our own species. On the contrary, it is known that in some places the two lived virtually side by side. As a result, the extinction of Neanderthal man is something of a puzzle. Of course just because the two species lived peacefully together in some places, does not mean that this was always the case. As the population of *H. sapiens* grew, there would have been competition for resources in those places where both species were to be found. It has been suggested that *H. sapiens* was more adaptable and that it could deal with rapidly fluctuating weather patterns better that the Neanderthals, but there is no real proof that this was the case. Also, being much more robust, Neanderthals needed more calories each day in order to survive, whilst *H. sapiens* could probably deal with periods of hardship better.

In terms of the final disappearance of Neanderthal man, there is no consensus and therefore a host of different suggestions. They may have been out-competed by *H. sapiens*, or even persecuted – and, knowing the capacity of modern humans for developing hatred for others on racial or religious grounds, this last possibility can surely not be ruled out. The simple fact is that we do not know, and although different parties will argue their point of view ferociously, no one hypothesis is presently any more likely or valid than any other.

This leaves the only hominid species presently inhabiting the Earth as our own. We are *Homo sapiens sapiens*, the pinnacle of hominid evolution and quite clearly the predominant species on our planet. There are now in excess of 7,000 million human beings alive in the world and the number shows no sign of diminishing. We have changed environments significantly, right across the planet, to suit our own needs, and no other species has ever utilized what the world has to offer to the extent that we have.

The first reliable evidence of modern humans from the fossil record is around 160,000 years old, but such is our scientific ability these days that we don't have to rely entirely on fossils when it comes to working out how long we have been around. In the last chapter we dealt with DNA, and it is this same substance that makes it possible for us to discover how far back in time our species stretches. In 1987 a study was carried out of nearly 200 human beings, living in various parts of the globe. What the scientists were keen to isolate was the mitochondrial DNA of the individuals concerned – mitochondrial DNA is inherited from our mothers. When the results were studied in detail, those running the experiment could be fairly sure of the conclusions. It was assessed that all modern human beings originate from Africa and that *Homo sapiens* appeared there about 200,000 years ago.

This research, and other studies that have taken place since, has proved to be extremely important in replacing the 'multiregional' theory of human

Millions of Years

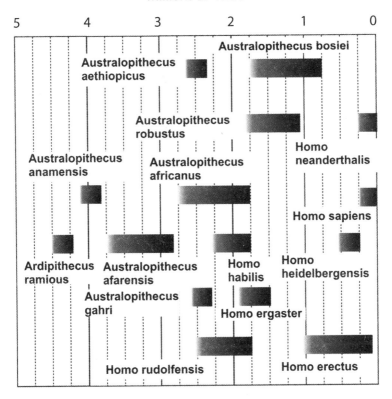

Comparison of the timescale of the genus *Homo*, its possible forebears
and other hominids

evolution, which suggested that *Homo sapiens* may have developed in
different parts of the world. There is now no longer any doubt. All of us
came ultimately from sub-Saharan Africa.

Since the oldest modern human skulls found so far date back only 160,000
years, there is a discrepancy between them and the DNA evidence, which
puts our origin back a further 40,000 years. This might be because we have
not yet found any fossil evidence that bridges the gap.

Bottlenecks

The origin and development of humanity is a line of research that has been of interest to me since my late teens and I have followed the progress of tracing our lineage ever since. With each new discovery, and every twist and turn, it became increasingly obvious to me that the missing link, which the Victorians and Edwardians were seeking, *is* still missing.

It might look at first sight as if the ascent of man is indeed now complete in the fossil record; after all, the latest hominids before the arrival of Neanderthal man and ourselves were not so very different to us. They were tall, had big brains, were organized and co-operative, and were tool-users. This last pre-human is typified by *Homo heidelbergensis*, who is an interesting character indeed. It might even be suggested that *H. heidelbergensis* was more superhuman than human because Professor Lee R Berger from the University of Witwatersrand, South Africa, carried out an extensive study of the bones of *H. heidelbergensis* and came to the conclusion that it was not uncommon for males of the species to be 2.13 metres in height! In imperial terms this is 7ft, which is exceptionally tall for a modern human male. In addition Professor Berger was able to show that these examples had been muscular in proportion to their size. This is huge indeed when one thinks of the tiny australopithecines that had been its ancestors.

However, the real missing link comes at around 2 million years ago, because prior to that time australopithecine species, with their smaller brains and much smaller frames, were successful across much of Africa. What is hard to discover is how these little ape-like creatures managed to turn themselves into the muscular, large-brained giants that appeared in the fossil record from around 2 million years ago.

Where anyone attempts an explanation, they usually put forward the theory of 'bottlenecking'. This suggests that large genetic changes can take place when a species is brought close to the brink of extinction, probably through some naturally occurring catastrophe that virtually wipes out a population. In particular I draw the reader's attention to the work of John

Hawks of the Department of Anthropology at the University of Utah, Keith Hunley from the University of Michigan, Sang-Hee Lee of the University for Advanced Studies at Kanagawa in Japan, and Milford Wolpoff, also of the University of Michigan.

Together, these men created a review entitled 'Population Bottlenecks and Pleistocene Human Evolution'. This is a very complicated report for all except the most knowledgeable experts, but a great deal of patient reading and referencing brings some very interesting facts to light.

It appears that many experts are now agreed that around 2 million years ago there was some sort of event that that led to a great step forward in the evolutionary progression of the hominid-type animals. It is at this point that the australopithecines begin to disappear, though there are exceptions, such as *Australopithecus boisei*, which continued on until around 750,000 years ago. However, generally speaking it is around the 2-million-year era that the genus *Homo* is identified. All of the creatures classified as being part of this genus are markedly more advanced than any of the australopithecines. In the case of creatures such as *H. ergaster* and *H. erectus* (which, incidentally, could be the same thing) the differences are extremely marked. These are not merely evident in terms of stature, skull characteristics, cranial capacity and the like, but also with regard to the complexity of behaviour and the success of the species beyond its starting point in Africa.

Writing about the relatively sudden appearance of the first species classifiable as *Homo,* Hawks, Hunley, Sang-Hee Lee and Wolpoff observe:

> We, like many others, interpret the anatomical evidence to
> show that early *H. sapiens* was significantly and dramatically
> different from earlier and penecontemporary australopithecines
> in virtually every element of its skeleton… Its appearance reflects
> a real acceleration of evolutionary change from the more slowly
> changing pace of australopithecine evolution.

A Genetic Revolution

A little further on they write:

> Our interpretation is that the changes are sudden and interrelated
> and reflect a bottleneck that was created because of the isolation of
> a small group from a parent australopithecine species. In this small
> population, a combination of drift and selection resulted in a radical
> transformation of allele frequencies, fundamentally shifting the
> adaptive complex... in other words, a genetic revolution.

Clearly not all australopithecines became *Homo* types, because we know that
the australopithecines continued to exist long after the new *Homo* genus
appeared, so it seems likely to me that the writers are correct in assuming that
the genus *Homo* developed from a fairly small group of australopithecines
and probably initially in an isolated location.

They suggest that, with perhaps a few exceptions, all members of the *Homo*
genus are less than 2 million years old and that as a result they are too recent
to be considered transitional forms of hominids leading to *H. sapiens*.

Hawks, Hunley, Sang-Hee Lee, and Wolpoff sum up the section of their
paper dealing with the differences between australopithecines and early *H.
sapiens* by saying:

> In sum, the earliest *H. sapiens* remains differ significantly from
> australopithecines in both size and anatomical details. Insofar as
> we can tell, the changes were sudden and not gradual.

They call what happened a *'genetic reorganization'* and go on to cite further
evidence, for example radical differences in behaviour. Bigger bodies, and
in particular bigger craniums and larger brains, require significantly more
calories per day in order to keep them going. The suggestion is that this fact
alone is a sure indication that the earliest members of the *Homo* genus were

meat eaters, and therefore hunters. The logic is that the supposed mainly vegetarian lifestyle of the australopithecines could not on its own have supported the very large creatures that the first *Homo* members had suddenly become. It is estimated that the 40–45 per cent increase in energy expenditure between australopithecines and early *Homo sapiens* would definitely have required a distribution of labour within a family or tribal group and a human-like foraging strategy.

The most telling paragraph of all in this report is:

> These behavioral changes are far more massive and sudden than any earlier changes known for hominids. They combine with the anatomical evidence to suggest significant genetic reorganization at the origin of *H. sapiens,* and from this genetic reorganization, we deduce that *H. sapiens* evolved from a small isolated australopithecine population and that small population size played a significant role in this evolution.

It is for all these reasons that a bottleneck is suggested in the case of the appearance of the *Homo*-type hominids. Why? because it is the only explanation at present that deals with all the issues. The writers of the report are of the opinion that the tremendous differences between the australopithecines and the early examples of the *Homo* genus are just too great and too sudden to be due to the routine processes of natural selection.

I am sure that the reader has grasped the significance of this situation already. The theory that some local disaster and a resultant bottleneck in the australopithecine population is a possible explanation, but it is not the only one. It is equally likely that a small and isolated population of australopithecines was targeted and that with a combination of selective breeding and maybe even genetic manipulation it was changed, very quickly, into an entirely different creature.

There are certainly many precedents for this. Dogs are a good example. It is likely that dogs attached themselves to human beings quite early because they share a similar life-style and the relationship between the two species has been mutually useful if not truly symbiotic. In all probability dogs did not change all that much for thousands of years, once they had been adopted by humanity to help with hunting and herding. However, during the last two or three hundred years a multitude of different dog types have appeared, all brought about as a result of selective breeding, often for reasons of pure fashion but also, in some cases, because of different intended uses of the animals. Despite the fantastic diversity, the smallest toy terrier could successfully mate with the largest Great Dane – if the obvious physical restraints were overcome. They are still the same species, in spite of their tremendous differences. It would be obvious to anyone that the differences between the Yorkshire terrier and the Great Dane are far greater than those between an australopithecine and a *Homo sapiens*, but they have been achieved in just a few centuries.

The same is true in breeds of pigs, sheep and cattle, as well as in chickens, ducks and a whole host of other creatures. Similar processes have taken place with plants, both those grown for display and for food.

Selective breeding can dramatically change the appearance and attributes of a species in just a few generations, and if we accept that human beings from the future have travelled regularly to the distant past, it is extremely likely that *their* intervention brought about the sudden change from australopithecine to *Homo*.

In a situation such as this there would be relatively few individuals involved. Whether or not we find fossil evidence of any creature is a game of numbers. For example, I can find endless examples on the local beach close to my own home of ammonite fossils because ammonites were extremely common during the Devonian and Cretaceous periods, and they proliferated for millions of years. In a dramatic change, such as that between australopithecines and the *Homo* genus, there would be relatively few creatures involved, so the chance of finding their fossil remains is that much less. As a result we may never happen across the results of the experiment as it was taking place – maybe across only a few generations. But this state of affairs would certainly explain a limited early gene pool for the *Homo* genus.

We already possess the skills to genetically manipulate creatures, including ourselves, and the possibility that such a thing took place two million years ago cannot be ruled out. The process may have been very much more than simple selective breeding, and with a little help from geneticists it is even possible that interbreeding between modern human beings and australopithecine took place.

Even closer to our own period there may have been intervention taking place in the later stages of human evolution. Led by evolutionary biologist Richard Dawkins, experts now agree that all of the existent humanity on our planet can be genetically traced back to a common female ancestor 140,000 years ago and a common male ancestor 60,000 years ago. Of course this does not mean that there literally ever was one single Eve or Adam, but it does serve to indicate that the population of human beings in the world was certainly not large in this remote period; it is a fact that, as a species, *Homo sapiens* is incredibly similar, right across the Earth. Any differences that do exist are superficial, as is demonstrated by the fact that human beings of any race or geographical origin can readily mate with any other.

At many stages in the early development of humanity it appears that only very small numbers of individuals were involved. In a world which has always been deeply competitive, such tiny populations of individuals as there appear to have been might have struggled to survive at all, though of course if they were being constantly nurtured, monitored and assisted, their eventual success would have been better assured. We see the same sort of situation taking place these days with regard to endangered species. Some creatures have been brought back from the very brink of extinction thanks to captive breeding programs. Other species survive *only* because of our intervention and the earliest true *Homo* genus may have been such a case.

No australopithecine and no other member of the *Homo* genus apart from our own presently exists, even in the remotest parts of our world. It is quite possible that in some cases we simply out-competed our cousins and they became extinct for this reason. But is it not equally likely that hominids were always going to represent a branch on the tree of life that would eventually come to an end? Perhaps, left to its own devices, the hominid family was always going to have low population levels and would eventually succumb to dramatic changes in climate or habitat.

In the case of *Homo sapiens* the saving grace was a huge brain, with the inherent adaptability and intelligence that this gave. Our brains are so large, and therefore our craniums so big, that birth is still an extremely precarious business for human mother and child alike – much more so than is the case with most other species. But it all worked and eventually saw us through to being the most influential species the Earth has ever known.

Such behaviour as would be necessary in order to safeguard, and even 'create', the creatures we would one day become is not at odds with the people we are right now. We already have the ability to 'manipulate' situations – to safeguard creatures that appeal to us in some way or which are useful, whilst being quite willing to eradicate those that pose a danger to humanity. Few people would mourn the passing of the *Anopheles* – the malaria mosquito that has been responsible for more human deaths than any other creature across history. This tiny but deadly creature is attacked ruthlessly wherever it appears.

Even a few decades ago the notion that modern humanity might have been effectively 'manufactured' would have seemed ridiculous, but we now have the ability to influence life at a very fundamental level. Such knowledge will not diminish, and the mind boggles at what we will be capable of achieving in just another generation or two. If even our present knowledge was harnessed to the ability to travel to the past, there is nothing about the sudden transformation of humanity from australopithecine to *Homo sapiens* that we could not bring about artificially in a relatively short period of time.

CHAPTER 6

Unidentified Future Objects

W alkers choosing to spend some time in Rendlesham Forest in Suffolk, England, may well come across a triangular information board. If they stop to read the words they will discover a report, by the Forestry Commission, of a series of supposed UFO sightings that took place in the vicinity back in 1980. They can then follow a deliberately created trail through the forest, which will take them along tracks and to clearings that featured in the events of December 1980.

Generally speaking, the British are quite stoical about such things and don't tend to make a great fuss, even over something as seemingly important as the visitation of aliens from some far distant star. For most of the year the forest remains quiet and the interested visitor will find little information available in the nearby towns and villages. It's a far cry from the souvenir shops, restaurants, book shops and the rest that are to be found across the Atlantic in America's most famous UFO town at Roswell, New Mexico. All the same, the Rendlesham Forest incidents have been called one of the most significant UFO happenings anywhere in the world. And what really sets the Rendlesham Forest incident apart is that it took place in an area that was just about as American as it was English. The incident began in the early hours of the morning of 26 December 1980. At the time this part of England was an especially sensitive location. The West was deep in the midst of the Cold War. Those of us who can recall the period will never forget that from the 1950s on, the bitterness and animosity that existed between the Soviet Union, and Western Europe and the USA sometimes reached fever pitch – with an underlying unease that at any time open aggression might be the result.

As a result of the accord that existed between the USA and Britain, American bases existed in several locations throughout the British Isles. Such was the case in Suffolk in 1980. The two sites in this part of Suffolk were RAF Bentwaters and RAF Woodbridge, both of which had formerly been used by the RAF during the Second World War. In the 1980s they were given over to the US Air Force. One or both of these bases had repositories of nuclear weapons and so they were well guarded.

The east gate of RAF Woodbridge faced out onto Rendlesham Forest, an area of dense woodland that lay between the base and the East Anglian coast. It was at this gate, around 3am on 26 December that a security patrol first saw lights emanating from the forest. There was sufficient concern for a security team to be sent into the forest. They reported strange lights moving amongst the trees and also a much brighter light emanating from some sort of craft. The report made by these first investigators suggests that after a while the craft took flight and disappeared.

It was from this first encounter that the testimony of Sgt Jim Patterson arose. Patterson is a controversial figure because others who were there at the time have no recollection of him being present, though he definitely did work at the base and was on duty at the time the incident took place. Patterson claims to this day that he encountered the craft. He took note of the fact that it had triangular landing gear, which left noticeable impressions on the forest floor once it had disappeared. Even more controversially, Sgt Patterson claims that he conversed with the occupants of the craft. He is adamant that they were not aliens, but rather time travellers from our own future. This is in stark contrast to the observations and opinions of most others who were present, all of whom remain adamant that the craft they saw *must* have been extraterrestrial in origin, though how anyone could make such a claim is something of a mystery.

One can imagine that those responsible for the base would be somewhat perturbed by these events. Security was tight and the threat from the Soviet Union was not taken lightly. Cases of spying were common and each side fought hard to retain its secrets and to hide its technology. It must have occurred to the base commanders that this would represent a very good period for the Soviets to mount some sort of covert spying mission because it was the Christmas holidays and many people were away from the base.

Early in the morning of 28 December the sightings from the camp began again. Once more a security team set off into the forest, this time led by Lt Col Charles I Halt, who was deputy commander of the base. Halt had a small tape recorder with him and kept up a verbal account of everything that took place, until the batteries gave out. This verbal testimony still exists and has been cited ever since as corroboration of the fact that something very strange was taking place. There are also claims by some of those who were present that a video tape was made at the time, but this has never been forthcoming since. What *is* known is that many still photographs were taken, which have also never been released.

Lt Col Halt and his men also saw coloured lights in the forest and encountered a strange craft amongst the trees. At the time, Halt's ability to openly report what he saw was hampered by the fact that he was a United States serviceman but since, in June 2010, Charles Halt, by this time retired, signed an affidavit that explained the events of the night in question, and which stated that in his opinion what he and his men had seen was of extraterrestrial origin.

The whole incident has been explained away by sceptics as being down to the existence of a lighthouse on the coast nearby at Orford Ness. They suggest that the flashing light from the lighthouse, shining through the trees, confused those present. They also note that some space debris entered the Earth's atmosphere that night, which may have added to the confusion.

Charles Halt is meanwhile adamant that neither had anything to do with what he and his party saw. He suggests that they were all aware of the lighthouse and that the lights they saw were well away from it. He had reported a large red light, like an eye, which moved in and out of the trees. He claims that it began to drip some substance, which looked like molten metal. This large red light eventually split into a number of smaller lights, and these he claimed flew away in different directions. He remains adamant that none of the lights reported were the lighthouse, which they were also monitoring at the time.

Information recently forthcoming from the British Ministry of Defence tends to suggest that the British authorities never took the situation seriously – or at least did not consider it to be a threat to national security. Those who endorse the sightings maintain that the Ministry is withholding the real information regarding the incidents. Meanwhile the American authorities have kept singularly quiet about the events in the Rendlesham Forest – though it is hard to see how they could have failed to instigate some sort of enquiry at the time.

It has to be remembered that the witnesses to these events were trained soldiers. They did not panic, and when interviewed, as they were by US agencies later, they gave a reliable account of what they had genuinely seen. The very fact that the United States authorities have never even verified that such interviews took place is bound to lead doubters to suggest that a cover-up has taken place, which probably involved the British Ministry of Defence.

It seems to me that anyone would be foolish to suggest that UFOs do not exist; the letters stand for 'Unidentified Flying Object', and since not every object that is seen in the sky can immediately or sometimes ever be identified, UFOs *must* exist. However, what most people mean when they use the letters UFO, is a flying craft of alien origin. For the existence of UFOs there is untold reliable evidence, whilst for the latter there is little that really stands up to scrutiny.

UFOs, whatever they might be, have often been seen by large groups of people simultaneously. Many have been filmed and the film or video tape has been carefully analysed to ensure that it is genuine. Aircraft pilots from around the globe have been seeing UFOs on a regular basis since at least the days of the Second World War. Civil pilots see them regularly too, though few such sightings are reported because the pilots concerned do not wish to subject themselves to ridicule or to make any report that might have an adverse bearing on their careers.

Ever since I was a child I have been puzzled and frequently amused to hear some of the suggestions made by so-called experts to explain away UFOs. The one that makes me laugh most is a chestnut that crops up all the time – namely that the observer was actually looking at the planet Venus. Even at its brightest, Venus looks like a star and it does not move haphazardly around the sky. Other explanations have been the Moon, which is even more unlikely than Venus; comets, which are usually reported in the media these days; together with more likely candidates such as military aircraft, weather balloons, strange-shaped clouds or meteorites and/or space debris re-entering Earth's atmosphere.

I happen to live in an area which is known as being a UFO hotspot. Close to my home is a large bay – in fact one of the largest in Britain. It is called Bridlington Bay and is the scene of countless UFO sightings each year. Doubtless most of these can be attributed to one of the explanations above, though many definitely cannot. Although I am interested in the subject I don't go out looking for UFOs, but I see them on a regular basis all the same. Because of my work and my past research, I know the night sky very well. I am familiar with most of the star patterns throughout the year, am aware of planets and can easily recognize high or low flying aircraft, which have very distinctive lights and which, even when at a very high altitude, make an audible sound as they pass over.

What I find more difficult to explain is the proliferation of triangular lights that appear extremely frequently in our local skies during darkness. The object (if that is what it is) always looks the same. There are three orange to red lights, forming the three points of a roughly equilateral triangle. These move noiselessly across the night sky and can travel in any direction, sometimes even changing direction quickly and retracing their previous flights, or going off at right angles. If these are craft it is impossible to say how large they are, because only the lights are visible. Neither can one ascertain the height of the objects, for the same reason. They often seem to move very quickly, but once again without any true point of reference it is impossible to say exactly what their speed might be.

Nobody who lives in this part of the world is surprised to see the triangular lights at any time. They can be observed over land or out at sea and sometimes a number appear in the same night. Friends have suggested that what we are probably seeing are Chinese lanterns, which are very popular these days, but this cannot be the case. Chinese lanterns have only one orange light and behave in a very different way. They are easy to spot and since they are so popular at the moment we have had many opportunities to do so.

Walking along the seafront of Bridlington Bay on almost any clear night, strange lights out at sea are a regular feature. Sometimes these are the same triangular configurations, but on other occasions they are single, white lights. Most frequently they travel along at some distance and just a little above the horizon. They often seem to move quite quickly, before suddenly stopping for a while, going back in the opposite direction or continuing their journey. My wife and I have observed such happenings for many minutes at a time. Indeed on one night the show went on for so long we became bored and cold, and walked home.

I cannot explain what any of these lights might be. That means as far as I am concerned they are definitely UFOs. Fortunately, I'm not alone because there are countless reports of such things in the area. Letters and articles regularly appear in the local papers and people have started to come here to visit the place, in the hope of catching a glimpse of a UFO.

What I do not automatically suggest is that what I am seeing are flying saucers or other sorts of craft from some alien world. How could I? I have no proof. They remain an enigma, as do most UFOs, and many may have a perfectly rational explanation. For all I know, this might be the case with the orange triangles – but I have yet to learn of one that seems remotely likely to me.

The fact is that, by far, the majority of UFOs are seen by normal, rational people who are simply going about their everyday business. When they give accounts, they do so in a truthful manner, though of course many simply do not report what they have seen to anyone, usually for fear of being ridiculed. I am sure there are also many people in the world who either fabricate accounts of UFO sightings, or who are easily fooled by a celestial or meteorological phenomenon that looks odd but is perfectly normal.

Generally speaking we do not go about looking up at the sky. That's a sure way to walk into a lamppost or to fall over a kerb. In fact the average person looks at the sky very little. With countless thousands of UFO sightings taking place around the world every year, common sense therefore asserts that only a small percentage of UFOs that are present are being seen by anyone.

Accounts of UFOs seen in daylight do not tend to vary all that much. Most common is the saucer or cigar-shaped object – which could be the same shape when either seen from below or from the side. This is the famed flying saucer that was first reported in the 1940s. Triangular craft of one sort or another are also very commonly reported, as are cylinders or tubes as some people call them. Many aircraft pilots have seen examples of all these types of craft up close.

Some of these were the pilots of F-94 night fighters, which were scrambled on the night of 17 July and early hours of 18 July 1952, to make contact with not one but a number of UFOs over Washington DC. Unfortunately, because of technical difficulties at Andrews Air Force Base, the jets took some time to get airborne. By the time they were aloft the UFOs had disappeared, but as soon as the F-94s landed again, the UFOs returned. There is reliable film of them flying in formation behind the Capitol – at least 12 in number. Often they flew at about 100mph, but when later chased by jet fighters they were observed to streak away at an estimated 7,000+mph, which is phenomenal.

These estimates were not made by the frustrated F-94 pilots, but by ground radar at both civil and military locations.

Pilots reported that the craft were saucer-shaped, which is borne out by close-ups made from the film footage and other photographs taken at the time. It soon became clear that the jets had no chance of catching the UFOs that seemed to be deliberately playing with them – allowing the aircraft to more or less get within firing range before speeding off in an instant.

Nor was this the last time Washington DC saw the UFOs because they returned on 26/27 July and provided another spectacular air display, proving once again that they could do more or less whatever they wished, with absolute impunity.

Hundreds if not thousands of people were aware of these two incidents. Not only the military but the civil aviation authorities recorded the antics of the UFOs on radar, and many ordinary citizens in Washington DC itself watched the display on both nights. So, bearing all this in mind, what was the explanation put forward by the authorities to mollify their agitated citizens? They suggested that the whole situation was due to temperature inversion.

Temperature inversion can cause lights on the ground to be reflected from the bottom of clouds. This can give the appearance of objects in the sky. It is a perfectly normal phenomenon but it can have had nothing to do with the two incidents in Washington DC. America's own Project Blue Book, which reported officially for years on UFO sightings, dismissed this explanation and no wonder. Jet fighters cannot chase temperature inversion, which would also not register on radar.

Those UFO watchers who are also fond of conspiracy theories claim that authorities around the world know a great deal more about UFOs than they are ever willing to admit, and though this may or may not be the case it is certainly a fact that information is often withheld; explanations are quite frequently absurd and those making reports of UFOs have often been either discredited or subjected to the most rigorous and sometimes even hostile interrogation. Perhaps governments around the world *do* know more than they are willing to admit, but it is also possible that their reaction is born out of frustration simply because they don't have a clue. People in power have a natural reticence to admit that they are in ignorance about anything – it just goes against the grain. In the comprehension of world leaders a mixture of ridicule and obfuscation may seem the best way to deal with something that is as much of a mystery to them as it is to the general public.

In addition to UFOs, there have been a massive number of reports of USOs. These are unidentified submerged objects and sightings of them seem to go back a lot further than the more traditional UFO. Such strange craft diving into the ocean, or appearing from it, go back to prehistory, though there are more contemporary and probably more reliable examples. One was reported in the newspapers in Malta, an island in the Mediterranean, back in the 19th century. On 18 June 1845 the sailing ship *Victoria* was east of Adalia in Turkey when its crew was astonished to see three luminous bodies appear from the ocean and take flight. The same objects were also seen from land in Adalia, other parts of Turkey and also Syria.

There are literally thousands of examples of USO encounters, seen from land, from ships and also from aircraft. Many of these describe objects, sometimes very large ones, that were seen entering or leaving bodies of water, to or from the sky. One of the best attested examples of a USO took place in Shag Harbour, Nova Scotia. On the night of 4 October 1967 at least 11 people, some of whom were at different locations and did not know each other, observed a large craft of some sort apparently crash into the sea just off Shag Harbour. The authorities took the reports very seriously, and thinking that an aircraft might have gone down, an intensive search-and-rescue mission was launched by the Canadian navy and air force. Immediately prior to the disappearance of the craft into the sea, countless people locally had seen UFOs in the area, and those who watched this disappearance beneath the waves suggested that the object in question was about 60ft in length and that a light remained visible on the water for some time after it submerged.

Naval vessels arrived and were able to confirm from sonar readings that something large was indeed positioned beneath the waters of Shag Harbour. After two days, no aircraft was reported missing, nothing happened beneath the water, and the authorities were just about to begin a salvage operation to try and recover the submerged object when a second USO appeared on the sonar and approached the first. There appeared to be some contact between the two craft and those observing waited with interest to see what would happen. Perhaps unfortunately some of the vessels engaged in the operation had to leave the location in order to intercept an approaching Russian submarine. The two submerged craft then made their way towards the Gulf of Maine, at this time remaining underwater. According to naval personnel who were interviewed at a later date, the two USOs then left the ocean and took to the sky again, disappearing rapidly.

The true import of this story may never be known. Much of the evidence for the later events in the unfolding drama came from retired military men who feared for their pensions, and so they were only willing to talk 'off record'. However, there were enough official reports at the time, as well as more concrete confirmation later, to demonstrate that something extremely odd happened in Canadian waters at that time.

Whether or not the authorities of the world are better informed than is the general public regarding the truth of UFOs and USOs, the sheer prevalence of such sightings demonstrates very clearly that something quite odd is going on. It has often been suggested that in the case of UFOs, many of the sightings can be put down to secret military projects, about which the public are kept deliberately in the dark. Doubtless this can indeed account for some sightings, but logic asserts that not all UFO appearances have anything to do with covert military projects. Putting aside simple mistakes and a host of perfectly natural phenomena that are misrepresented by witnesses, there is still a large percentage of sightings every day by sensible, sane people who would not be easily fooled.

If even a percentage of UFO sightings represents craft of some sort, directed by intelligent beings, it is clear that they have nothing to fear from us because their technology is so in advance of our own that there is no comparison. The behaviour of the UFOs in Washington DC in 1952 would seem to indicate that those controlling the craft either 'test' our capabilities or simply have a well developed sense of humour. But if the operators of UFOs have nothing to fear from us, it seems to me that neither do we have anything to fear from them. If all the observation of humanity that is apparently taking place is the precursor to some sort of invasion, those concerned are certainly taking their time. Since they outmatch us so much in a technological sense, it appears self-evident that they could take over our planet at any time they wished.

Rather, one gets the impression that we are being carefully watched. The appearance of so many USOs might indicate that such surveillance craft are present most of the time and that their operators deliberately choose to make their bases below the oceans, where in the main it would be easy for them to avoid detection. Not that those responsible appear to be all that troubled about being seen. With the level of expertise and technology that is demonstrated by the manoeuvrability and agility of UFOs, one would imagine that those responsible could, if they so wished, employ some sort of cloaking device that would make their craft as good as invisible. Our own military technology is not too far away from this highly desired objective. UFOs are regularly captured on radar, whilst the most modern stealth fighters remain invisible to detection by design.

It is worthwhile drawing a few strings together regarding UFOs. In order to do so we will first have to conjecture that at least some of these are deliberately engineered craft, operated by intelligent beings.

- UFOs are not, in the main, hostile.
- UFOs are clearly technologically more advanced than our own craft.
- Those operating UFOs do not go to any great trouble to hide their presence.
- Since there is no hostility, bearing in mind the frequency of UFO sightings, we can take it that those responsible are monitoring us.

- The more technologically adept we have become, the greater have been the observed occurrences of UFO activity.

I would argue that if UFOs are a reality, in terms of being deliberately engineered craft designed to observe what is taking place on the Earth, it is far more likely that they *come from* the Earth rather than from any of our companion stars. The sheer frequency alone indicates that there is nothing casual or limited about UFO activity. For any alien species to have as many craft operating constantly, so far from home, would represent a mammoth exercise – and for what purpose? Any culture that was advanced enough to cross interstellar space could create observational devices that could be present on the Earth all the time.

Even more likely is the fact that, if we are genuinely being watched by our cousins from far away, they would wish to make contact with us. There are indeed examples of encounters of the 'third kind', but these represent a very small proportion of UFO sightings and are often quite suspect. When everything is taken into account and when one remembers, as I pointed out in Chapter Two, just how unlikely it is that any advanced civilization would be around in our part of space at this specific time, the idea of visitors from other worlds is extremely unlikely.

So, if at least some UFO encounters represent craft that come from our own future, what is the purpose of such visits? The first possibility that occurs to me also seems to be the most likely. What historian, given the opportunity, would pass up the chance to see at first hand the events in which he or she is so interested? It seems unlikely that our natural curiosity is likely to diminish at any time soon and it may be that our future selves choose to return to our time and view what is going on here – simply because they can do so.

What is interesting is that the frequency of UFO sightings is increasing all the time. There are examples from remote history, but it has been during our own technological era, especially since the 1940s, that UFO activity has proliferated. Certainly, we monitor our own skies much more these days than we did in the past and, of course, with a massive increase in world population, there are also many more people around who *can* see UFOs. There was a tremendous amount of UFO activity during the Second World War and throughout the Cold War that followed, and it is slightly strange how often such activity seems to increase at the time of catastrophes and also during human conflict. This might simply reflect the curiosity of our future selves.

As I hope to demonstrate presently, it may not be long before the suggestions I am making in this book become obvious to everyone. It could be that in the build-up to our realization that our past has been heavily influenced by our future, visitations become more frequent, together with the interventions such activity implies.

Bearing in mind the sheer number of UFOs that have been seen over the years, it isn't beyond the realms of credibility that our future selves keep more or less permanent bases in our own time. The oceans of the world are vast and, in places, extremely deep. It's an oft-quoted truism that we know more about space than we do about the world's watery depths, and it would be relatively easy for any truly advanced visitors to live almost indefinitely below the oceans – and without necessarily being detected. If this is the case, many of the UFOs that appear around the globe could simply be 'scout' ships, from much larger underwater bases.

A less obvious reason for so much UFO activity during the present era might be related to an increasing need on the part of our future selves to keep us 'plugged in and interested'. As we approach 'first contact' with our future selves – and when any pretence or secrecy is dropped for good – we need to be prepared for what is to come. This will take a degree of conditioning for what will prove to be an extremely surprising and for some a quite frightening reality. What is not at all likely is that, without any prior warning, someone will appear on the podium at the United Nations to tell the assembled delegates what has really been going on. People need to be brought to the truth slowly and steadily, to avoid panic and to allow religious leaders and philosophers to deal with the complexity of issues that such knowledge will create.

Could it even be that the reason the authorities around the world are so willing to limit the truth regarding UFO encounters is because at some level they already know what is taking place?

To a great extent books, television programmes and especially movies are already making us party to possibilities that only a few decades ago would have made no sense whatsoever. Technology is ripping ahead at a fantastic pace – so fast, in fact, that we can never be certain how many of our advances and discoveries are in some way influenced or aided by interventions from the future. One might get the sense that we are being deliberately 'brought up to speed', whilst at the same time being prepared for what is surely still going to be the biggest shock humanity has ever faced.

Nor can we dismiss the possibility that so many UFO sightings are taking place at this time as a consequence of the fact that so many individual human beings are under the direct influence of our future selves. This is not only possible but, as I intend to show in the next chapter, is extremely likely.

CHAPTER 7

Manipulation

About 25 years ago I was having a shower one day when I noticed a lump on my right forearm that I had not registered previously. It wasn't especially large and was not sore or irritating, but because it is wise to monitor such things I mentioned it to my physician. He was somewhat puzzled by the lump and thought it best to send me to the local hospital, so it could be examined properly.

After looking carefully at the lump, the doctor at the hospital thought it useful to have my arm X-rayed. The result only increased the mystery because it was clear from the picture that within the mass was some sort of foreign body that showed up bright white. A surgeon was called and within a few minutes a small incision had been made and the lump was removed. Whatever was within my arm had been there for quite some time, because my body had built tissue around it. When this was dissected with great difficulty it was found to contain a small piece of what looked like metal, probably about three or four millimetres in length and maybe a millimetre across – about the size of a piece of pencil lead.

I used to be a hands-on engineer and I know very well just how troublesome metal fragments can be if they get under the skin. Like me, the surgeon was puzzled that such a relatively large piece of metal had not been attacked by my immune system and neither had it set up an infection within my arm. There was no sign of a point of entry, though in fairness this could have disappeared because the metal fragment might have been there for years. The situation remained a mystery, but I had the wound stitched and once my arm was healed I thought little more about my strange passenger. What I certainly did not do was to request that I might keep the metal fragment, which I now regret.

In the last chapter I dealt with UFOs and the possibility that some sightings may be as a result of visitations to our time frame of people from the future. What I did not mention was the thorny subject of supposed alien abduction and implants, in which unsuspecting people are apparently 'probed' in some way by agencies from elsewhere. Although I have been aware of this topic for many years, it is something I have always tried to sideline because it looks at first sight to be the province of irrational individuals. The whole business seems highly unlikely and, in any case, I told myself that a large proportion of such supposed incidents were probably down to strange dreams, a desire on the part of some people to attract attention to themselves, or even simple hysteria. I most certainly did not place myself in this category and would probably have never done so had it not been for the fact that I came across the work of Dr Roger Leir.

Dr Leir is a podiatric surgeon, who has been in private practice in California, USA, for the last 43 years. It was his work as a podiatric surgeon that led him to begin wondering about a particular type of object that turned up in a few of his patients – sometimes in the wake of a report by the individual concerned of some sort of abduction. Having removed several foreign bodies such as the one in my arm (or been present when they were removed) and noticing that there were significant similarities between cases, Dr Leir, who is a naturally curious individual, was eventually forced to ask himself whether there might be some validity in the stories a few of his patients were telling him. As a result, he began to take more notice of the objects themselves.

I made it my business to get hold of a television documentary in which Dr Leir took part. Included in the footage was an operation in which such a foreign body was removed. The size and shape of the object, together with

Dr Leir's testimony as to the way the patient's system had reacted to it, took my mind back to my own experience and I decided that, no matter how unlikely the whole situation might be, I should look further into the subject.

Some of the objects removed by Dr Leir or his colleagues tend to be fairly similar to the one in my own arm, but as Leir became more and more intrigued by their occurrence he enlisted the support of other agencies to try and determine the true nature of the objects. Some of the laboratories he has called upon are extremely prestigious, for example those at Los Alamos National labs, Seal laboratories, the University of California at San Diego and New Mexico Tech. On many occasions, those examining the fragments have been mystified as to their composition and origin. Comparisons have been made between such fragments and material from meteorites, and samples have been found to contain strange, highly magnetic iron that, almost unbelievably, has no crystalline structure. In addition, some of the fragments have isotope ratios demonstrating that they are composed of substances that had not originated in our part of space and which are not natural in origin.[2] In other words, they appear to have been deliberately manufactured.

Dr Leir learned to be meticulous in his removal and examination of the fragments found in his patients. What sets his work apart is that he has always followed an entirely scientific procedure in his investigations. There was always a team of specialist observers present during the procedures and scrupulous notes, photographic and film records were kept.

If we were to assume for a moment (which I have never done in the past) that some of the abductions, or at least the implantation episodes, were genuine, we might then try to explain them in light of the intervention theory.

One of the most important observations Leir has made is that in many cases the 'implant' was connected to a 'mat' of nerve endings within the tissue of the subjects. This of course would connect it directly to the central nervous system and ultimately the brain of those involved. Unless the device is actually doing something that is intended, it seems unlikely that the body would react in this way to a foreign object. However, if the device was specifically created to serve as some sort of communication device, a direct connection with the brain of the subject would make eminent sense.

It is true that the objects in question are extremely small, but I would certainly not dismiss their possible significance on these grounds. As I go about my day-to-day business, in particular as I travel around the world to conferences and seminars, I often need to take a great deal of information with me. It isn't always convenient to carry a laptop, but in any case it isn't usually necessary these days because I never go anywhere without a USB memory stick. The latest example I have has 16GB of memory, which in terms of, for example, Word documents, would be enough to hold a significant library of information and yet it is smaller than the average postage stamp.

I am told by my computer wizard friends that USB memory sticks could easily be smaller, but there comes a point beyond which diminutive size is a disadvantage. In other words, we have to 'find' the stick in our pocket or bag and then we have to manipulate it into the USB slot of a computer. I may be wrong, but I would not be surprised to learn that electronic storage or surveillance devices of some complexity already exist (most probably in military circles) that are not much bigger than the fragments taken from the limbs of Dr Leir's patients or indeed from my own arm. Bearing in mind the way technology progresses, and in particular miniaturization, what I can say with absolute certainty is that if such small devices do not exist right now, it will only be a short time before they do.

Since such a device could connect itself to the brain of the subject, via the central nervous system, it would not require batteries of any kind. Human beings have their own in-built power supply because our whole nervous system runs on electricity – albeit at a very low voltage. What I am suggesting is that if these devices are real, and if someone is implanting them in us, they have been cunningly created so as to ensure that the host into which they are placed unwittingly looks after their tiny electrical requirements.

So, taking things one stage further, if at least some implant devices are real, what is their intended purpose? Logic asserts that they would either be used to get information 'into' or 'out of' an individual – or possibly both. In this sense they could act as a homing device, or perhaps even a 'window on the past' for humans living in the near or remote future. It might even be possible for those receiving the information sent by the implants to see what the subjects see, and even hear what they hear, in a moment-by-moment sense. Such information could be transmitted by the device, though it has to be admitted that as things stand in electronics right now, with such a tiny object the thought of signals being transmitted over any great distance seems unlikely. But this may not be relevant. We are, after all, talking about the future and even the most diehard sceptic would be forced to admit that the way things are proceeding in the field of microscopic engineering, almost anything seems possible. Already scientists at the Max Planck Institute of Quantum Optics have succeeded in storing quantum information on a single atom. And since, as we have seen, in the quantum world it is possible for particles to exist in many places simultaneously, further advances will surely lead to ever new and better ways of transmitting and receiving information in the universe of the extremely small.

Watchers from the future receiving information from a chosen subject in this way would in no way contradict the intervention theory, since they would not be attempting to alter the past, simply to observe it. One of the main reasons for indulging in this sort of clandestine 'snooping' could be nothing more than curiosity. As I have pointed out, I, for example, am fascinated by history at almost every level and I would be over the moon if I was given the chance to look in on the Battle of Hastings, or further back to the building of the pyramids or structures such as Stonehenge, through the eyes of someone present. How much we could learn in this way and although the technique is invasive, in most cases the subject would never be aware that anything unusual was taking place. In theory, hundreds or even thousands of people alive today, or in the past, could have spent their whole lives with such devices living harmlessly inside them, like so many surveillance cameras, offering our future selves the most incredible insight into specific events or even routine life across millennia.

Such a procedure would make sense. Everyone in physics agrees that time travel, if it ever takes place at all, is going to be extremely difficult and very expensive. Keeping significant numbers of any given generation of people from the past 'on line' and carrying devices in their bodies would mean that our future selves could probably keep track of what was happening at any given time, without having to be there personally. The initial journeys undertaken to any time period could be for the purpose of implanting the devices.

If information could be transmitted by such a device, and bearing in mind the veritable web of nerve endings that Dr Leir has found attached to them, it is more than likely that the information highway provided by them could be working in two directions. What I mean by this is that the devices could be specifically created to ensure that signals sent *to* the implants could be received by the brain of the subject. He or she could be totally unaware that such a situation was taking place. Suggestions, and even direct instructions, might be designed to proceed to subconscious areas of the brain – well away from the reasoning centres of subjects. This could provide the 'guinea pigs' with information they did not know they possessed. They could be implanted with false memories or even obliged to take specific actions that they would not have thought of undertaking otherwise.

I am aware that such a hypothesis will alarm some people, though I have to admit that I am personally sanguine about the prospect. Firstly, if I was such a subject, there would nothing I could do about it. Secondly, we have to bear in mind that under the limitations of intervention theory and the Novikov self-consistency principle, I could not be made to do anything that did not ultimately take place. We have to remember that events from the past cannot be changed – they can only be confirmed. It would therefore be pointless for our future selves to try and make a subject rob a bank or shoot a political leader – unless this is what had actually happened and was written in the annals of history.

As I look back at the broad spectrum of history, I can easily see a range of people whose lives and actions seemed diametrically at odds with their period and surroundings. A good example of such an individual would be Leonardo da Vinci, who lived between 1452 and 1519 in Italy and latterly in France. Most people know that he was a superlative artist, both in terms of painting and sculpture. He created masterpieces such as the famed *Mona Lisa* and *The Last Supper*.

Art was only the tip of the iceberg as far as da Vinci was concerned; he had an incredible curiosity. He was involved in subjects as apparently unrelated as the dissection of human cadavers in order to better understand anatomy, and the creation of state-of-the-art weaponry. There was not a branch of science that did not utterly fascinate him, even though science in the modern sense of the word did not exist at the time. He constantly kept notebooks, most of which were written in a sort of mirror code, many of which have not survived. Those notebooks that have stood the test of time indicate a man whose knowledge was way beyond anything seen elsewhere in his own day. Da Vinci's knowledge of optics, flight, engineering, chemistry and a host of other subjects was at least in tune with discoveries and observations made in the 18th, 19th and in some cases the 20th centuries. He would undoubtedly have been the most famous inventor who has ever lived, were it not for the fact that his own era could not provide the technology or materials that his proposals demanded.

Having been fascinated with da Vinci for decades, I have often asked myself, as an engineer, whether I could have achieved as much as he did if I was to be placed, with my present knowledge, in 15th-century Europe. I am forced to conclude that I could not have done half as well – even aside from the fact that I am no artist. The period of the European Renaissance was a wonderful era, with ideas exploding all over the place. But raw technology, especially in terms of materials, had to catch up and this took a very long time. For example, it is one thing being able to conceive of the forces that make a helicopter fly, as Leonardo quite definitely did, but something very different finding anything akin to titanium steel or carbon fibre in his own backyard to make the theory into reality.

Da Vinci was an ideas machine. It was as if he was a conduit for a host of scientific discoveries that would not occur again for centuries. All were funnelled through his brain, but in so many cases the result was utter frustration. He could see what needed to be done, but had no way to do it.

If we were to suppose that the fantastic knowledge possessed by Master Leonardo was sent direct to his brain from the future, we would also have to ask ourselves why this had taken place? The answer is quite simple – our future selves only had to look at their own history books to see what Leonardo had been capable of achieving, at least theoretically. All that remained was to implant him as a child and to gradually fill his head with everything that spilled out across the next 60 years.

Looking back at history there are any number of individuals who fall into the same general category as da Vinci. In the realms of science we might name Archimedes, Frances Bacon, Albert Magnus, Galileo, Newton and even Einstein, to mention only a few. A really good example might be the little-known German chemist, Friedrich August Kekulé (1829–96). Kekulé's great contribution to science was that he was a principal discoverer of the theory of chemical structures. This might not sound all that impressive, but everything that followed in chemistry was in some way dependent on Kekulé's descriptions.

Kekulé somehow understood the way atoms bond in molecules, and his greatest claim to fame is the work he undertook on benzene rings. Benzene had been known for decades. It is a volatile liquid obtained from coal tar and it has a somewhat complicated composition. Around 1862 Kekulé was able to describe the make-up of benzene as a six-membered ring of carbon with alternating single and double bonds. Although Kekulé was clearly a genius in the world of chemistry, he was extremely modest regarding his most famous discovery. Years later he claimed that the whole notion had come to him in the form of a daydream, in which he visualized a snake consuming its own tail. Whilst it is true that chemistry was undergoing great changes at this period of European history, the very nature of Kekulé's realization has all the hallmarks of messages sent from elsewhere and regurgitated from his subconscious mind.

Without wishing to detract in any way from years of patient, diligent study, there have been moments in the lives of many people of science in which sudden realizations have led to dramatic consequences. What is more, this might have taken place far more often than we realize. There is one particular character from history who, to my way of thinking, typifies the possibility of 'implant manipulation' more than any other. His name was Thomas Jefferson (1743–1826) third President of the United States of America. In addition to his political success he was also a writer, thinker, architect and scientist extraordinary.

Even before I began to contemplate the possibility of implantation, I was certain that Thomas Jefferson was manipulated on not one but many levels during his life, and for a number of different reasons. There were interludes during his years both as a statesman and a private citizen when it is clear that he was in possession of extremely potent information he should logically not have possessed – though in all probability he may not have even realized that this was the case.

The initial reason that my colleague Chris Knight and I focused so much of our attention on Thomas Jefferson was because of his skills as a metrologist. As Secretary of State of the United States, in 1790 Jefferson approached Congress with the idea of the new United States introducing a completely new and revolutionary series of integrated measuring systems. When we studied Jefferson's suggestions, Chris and I soon came to realize that incorporated within them were elements of a measuring system we had rediscovered from prehistory. I will mention more about this system in a later chapter but suffice it to say, as far as we were concerned, until that point in time the Megalithic measuring system had disappeared from history as early as around 1700BC.

If this was the only reason for thinking Jefferson's actions were being 'directed' by some outside source, we may have put the whole situation down to some bizarre though extremely unlikely coincidence. However, Jefferson's actions regarding measuring systems were incidental to the part he had to play in the building of America, and by implication the modern world. In his own way Thomas Jefferson was as much of a polymath as Leonardo da Vinci. He was a startling mathematician, an expert surveyor, a talented architect and an adept inventor; but if there is one aspect that sets this man apart from his peers and the age in which he lived, it is the words he spoke and wrote.

Jefferson penned most of the words of the American Declaration of Independence, which is a sterling expression of a way of thinking that was truly revolutionary at the end of the 18th century. His handling of such an important document was brilliant enough, but for the remainder of his life his observations on religion, philosophy, economics and politics betray a genius that sets him quite apart, even from the other inspirational characters who formed the nucleus of the Founding Fathers.

As I will show, it becomes increasingly clear that Thomas Jefferson was also a leading light when it came to the planning and building of Washington DC, a city and a subject that is more important to my ideas regarding intervention than just about anything else. There is no doubt in my mind that if manipulation from the future is a reality (and I become more certain that it is) Jefferson is the most startling example of manipulation at work that I have ever come across.

Dr Leir, who is just about the only individual presently taking the idea of implants seriously, takes the trouble to have both hypnotists and psychologists present when an object is removed from any of his subjects. The subjects themselves are always questioned as to whether they could remember any strange incident that might have had a bearing on the situation. In many cases there were half-remembered incidents of encounters with strange lights, unusual objects or shadowy figures. One subject recalled lying in bed and being aware of a strange light beyond the bedroom window. Others reported being involved in journeys in which a UFO sighting had taken place, and many reported incidents in which periods of time had 'gone missing' from their consciousness.

So what about my own experience? Whilst I certainly do not remember strange operating theatres, alien figures or journeys to far-off places, as some individuals in the field of UFO abduction claim to do, there was an incident many years ago that could tie up with my own 'implant' – at least I think there was. One of the problems with human memory is that it can be so easily fooled. It has been shown in tests that a specific television programme, something read in a book or even heard in a conversation, can be taken on board and incorporated into something we are certain really did happen to us, even though it could never have done so. That is why I have always dismissed my own personal close encounter as being nothing more than an unintentional fabrication, though perhaps this is not the case at all.

When I was young I was a keen boy scout and, like my peers, I was always seeking to increase the number of 'proficiency badges' I could display on the arm of my uniform shirt. On one occasion, when I would have been about 11 or 12 years of age, I embarked on a journey that would win me another, this time for a 10-mile hike. I undertook the hike with another scout and it took place one early spring Saturday. We were to walk from the town of Ilkley in Yorkshire, to Otley, and our journey would take us across remote moors, high above the beautiful valley of Wharfedale.

The walk went well and David and I steadily climbed to the highest point on our journey, where we decided to stop and have our lunch. It was rather blustery, so we took shelter behind one of the many dry-stone walls that crisscross even the highest uplands in northern England. There we sat and unpacked our sandwiches. I can clearly remember that as we ate and chatted, suddenly, and without any hint of a sound, an extremely large and impressive UFO came from behind us. We could not have monitored its approach because of the wall, but in an instant, there it was. In my mind's eye I can still see it clearly. It was shiny and metallic, glinting in the sun and about as typical of a classical flying saucer as it is possible to be. The craft carried no markings, though it did have several indentations and protrusions, some of which could have been hatches or ancillary equipment. I do not recall any lights, but in my memory the object was extremely close – probably not more than 50 feet or so above the ground; certainly close enough to cast a sizeable shadow onto the heather around us.

And that is it – the end of my memories regarding this peculiar experience. Did it ever really happen? I always told myself, even when I was younger, that it could not have genuinely taken place. I do not remember discussing it at the time with my companion, when surely such an amazing encounter would have been talked about avidly all the way home? Nor do I recall the craft moving away. It wasn't there – then it was, and then the memory ends.

I replay this event, if indeed it ever was an event, in all sincerity and just as it remains in my consciousness. It turns out that this is quite typical of many accounts of supposed abductions and implantations. What remains, in so many cases, are nothing more than half-remembered events, as if the subjects are not intended to have full recall about what took place. Are my memories of that long-gone day associated in some way with the object that was removed from my arm a decade and a half later? I cannot say for sure. I have certainly talked about the close encounter that David and I had on that lonely moor many times during my life, but I have never been absolutely certain that anything really took place. Quizzing David many years later it was obvious that he remembered less than I do. He recalled stopping to have lunch beside the wall, but then could remember nothing until we were once more walking.

What I do have are four tiny scars on my forearm, a legacy of the stitches that closed the wound once the strange little object was removed. I also have an insatiable curiosity – a need to know what makes the world tick, and I have been lucky enough to virtually 'trip over' a host of clues that have allowed me, both on my own and together with Chris Knight, to uncover aspects of our common human past that have been lost for thousands of years. I cannot explain where many of the original hunches came from that ultimately led to some of our most amazing, provable discoveries. Many of them seem like the snake chasing its tail that led to Friedrich August Kekulé describing benzene rings – they just arrived unbidden. In the common language of our partnership, Chris and I have always thanked what we refer to as 'the library angels'. This is a term we invented to try and explain those so-weird moments when the truth of a situation literally landed in our laps.

I cannot escape the possibility that I may have been implanted with a device from the future when I was still a boy, and even its eventual discovery and removal may have been deliberately planned. Our future selves have all the cards in their hands. For example, they have access to the very book you are reading now. The knowledge this offers them, taken together with the ability to travel back in time, allows them to 'make' history into the reality it must become. I do not believe that this is simply a sort of temporal voyeurism. Individually, specific events of UFO sightings or supposed implantation might not seem to be particularly important, but collectively they contribute to the dawning of awareness on the part of humanity that one day these events *will* take place. If there had been no clues, such as my own experiences and discoveries, or the remarkable insights of people such as da Vinci or Thomas Jefferson, we would have remained ignorant of something we simply have to know.

There is absolutely no doubt that the present is the launching pad of the future. As I hope to demonstrate, that future *must* include time travel. If it did not, it is doubtful that even the most primitive form of life would ever have developed on our world and it is certain that humanity would not have evolved. As we shall see, humanity is 100 per cent responsible for its own existence. What is more, were it not for the truly remarkable species that we are, the Earth would undoubtedly be nothing more than a solid and lifeless rock, spinning crazily around an anonymous sun, in one of the spiral arms of a fairly unremarkable galaxy.

CHAPTER 8

Measure for Measure

I am well aware that the evidence I have presented until this point could be considered conjectural. It was born of careful observation, but in most cases there is more than one way of looking at any individual situation. What I have sought to present is the most likely scenario, based on a balance of probabilities. We now move into a very different kind of evidence, which represents my own work and that of Chris Knight, for the last 20 years. This research has resulted in five books and is unambiguous in its implications, but it began in a very simple way – because we sought to rescue the reputation of an individual we thought had been vilified by archaeologists. In so doing we inadvertently opened up a seam of evidence that is revolutionary in the study of ancient history.

The person in question was Professor Alexander Thom. This truly remarkable man was born in Scotland in 1894. Known to his friends as 'Sandy', Alexander Thom was a bright boy who showed an early interest in mathematics and astronomy. Ultimately he would become Professor of Engineering at Oxford University, but a series of early observations in his native Scotland led to a lifetime of diligent study into a field that was not his chosen career.

Thom was a keen yachtsman and during his forays around the coast and lochs of Scotland he regularly encountered the proliferation of Megalithic standing stone circles and alignments that dot the mainland and islands of his homeland. He examined many of these closely and, taken together with his interest in astronomy, he looked at them in a very different way to most observers. He began to conjecture that many of these structures, most of which are at least 4,000 years old, may have been devices deliberately created to track and therefore understand the tortuous movements of the Moon. Like Alexander Thom himself, our late Stone-Age and Bronze-Age ancestors were good sailors. An understanding of the Moon's behaviour would have been invaluable to them in their maritime pursuits, so it seemed only natural to Thom that they would have shown an interest. Of course belief is not proof, so working entirely in his spare time, Thom set out to discover whether at least some of the Megalithic structures in both the British Isles and Brittany did have an astronomical purpose.

For upward of 50 years, working alone and also with family and friends, Thom carefully surveyed and measured as many Megalithic monuments as he could. By the end of his long life he had amassed data on literally hundreds of sites. He was able to show that many of the Scottish circles had a strong lunar connection, and if his endeavours had stopped at this conclusion he would be revered to this day by astroarchaeologists (a study he virtually invented). Unfortunately for his reputation, Thom felt obliged to publish *everything* he discovered, and one particular consequence of his research would lead to criticism, ridicule and even accusations of tampering with his results by some individuals.

The fly in the ointment, as far as Thom was concerned, was that he soon became aware that a particular linear unit began to drop out of his figures. It was evident to him that those who had created the Megalithic masterpieces, from the north of Scotland, right down to Brittany, had used a common measurement. Thom declared this to be 2.722 feet in length (82.966cm) and he christened it the Megalithic Yard. What was even worse was that the statistics of all his measurements showed that the Megalithic Yard was accurate to an incredible degree, from site to site across the whole area in which he worked. Almost from the start this got him into trouble with some of his contemporaries, and for good reason. What they found difficult to understand was how a particular unit of measurement could have been preserved and passed on with such stunning accuracy, across more than 2,000 years and over such a wide geographical distribution at such an early period.

In some of his published work Thom struggled to make sense of the Megalithic Yard. He admitted that to keep a 'sample' measure, one that could be passed on from generation to generation and across such a large area, would have been difficult, if not impossible. Nevertheless, he was a very capable statistician and a meticulous surveyor. He might not have been able to explain how the Megalithic Yard was reproduced with such stunning accuracy, but the figures did not lie, and like the good scientist he was he allowed his results to speak. Until the time of his death, in 1985, he continued to believe that the Megalithic Yard must be a reality. He went even further and suggested that a longer unit, which was equal to 2.5 Megalithic Yards, had also been used. This he called the Megalithic Rod. Its existence also demonstrated that the Megalithic builders were familiar with and undoubtedly also used the half Megalithic Yard. Studying some of the rock carvings left by the same people, Thom also suggested that the Megalithic Yard had been split into 40 smaller units, which he called Megalithic Inches.

Chris Knight and I thought it a great shame that such a meticulous man should have his reputation sullied, particularly since many of those who suggested he was deluded or simply mistaken were neither mathematicians nor engineers. As a result we decided to look closely at the Megalithic Yard, to try and establish if it had existed and if so, how it had been kept so accurate at a time when technology was quite limited.

Our own journey to understanding was quite long, but nowhere near as long as that of the ever patient Alexander Thom. What we ultimately discovered was that the Megalithic Yard had never been kept as a sample measure in wood or stone that could be passed on from generation to generation. Rather it had been recreated from scratch wherever it was needed. This was achieved by way of the simplest machine imaginable – a pendulum, together with an observation of a particular object in the night sky. For those who are interested and who have not read our previous books, the proof of our findings are included in Appendix 1 of this book.

The existence of the Megalithic Yard proved to be a key that opened a door on an ancient form of geometry and an integrated measuring system that was incredible in its accuracy. By comparing the Megalithic Yard with another known measurement from the same period, we were eventually able to show that our ancient ancestors were much, much brighter than anyone had ever realized. The alternative linear measurement came from the Minoan civilization on the Mediterranean island of Crete. The Minoans were contemporary with the Megalithic cultures of the British Isles and represent Europe's first super-civilization. Their linear measurement, used in the construction of many palaces and other buildings, the ruins of which still exist, was just under a modern statute foot of 30.48cm. The Minoan Foot measured 30.365cm. With the aid of the Minoan Foot, the Megalithic Yard and a wonderful clay disc from Crete which is known as the Phaistos Disc, we were eventually able to recreate the Earth geometry of which both these linear units had been a part.

Neither of these linear measurements existed in isolation; both are ultimately based on the polar circumference of the Earth therefore being what are known as 'geodetic' measurements. They are part of a lost form of geometry, which itself was allied to a ritual yearly calendar of 366 days. In this form of geometry there were 366° to the circle, and not the 360° we are familiar with these days. In Megalithic geometry, as we came to call it, each degree was split into 60 smaller units (Megalithic minutes of arc) and each minute of arc was split into 6 smaller units still (Megalithic seconds of arc). In terms of the polar circumference of the Earth and judging the Earth to be a circle, each Megalithic second of arc was equal to 366 Megalithic Yards. This result is frighteningly accurate and leaves me speechless even today.

Our first proof that the Megalithic second of arc of the polar circumference of the Earth was a genuine unit was the fact that 1,000 Minoan Feet and 366

Megalithic Yards are exactly the same thing. They were alternative units of linear measurement, but together they confirmed the existence of 366° geometry.[3]

Once we had uncovered the lost Megalithic geometry, the floodgates were open and all sorts of incredible discoveries appeared. We came to realize that although the Megalithic Yard had disappeared (most likely by 1700BC) other units of measurement still used in the world had originally been derived from it. For example, we realized that a cube with sides of 1/10th of the Megalithic Yard would hold exactly 1 pint of water.[4] Further to this, if the same cube is filled with any kind of cereal grain, for example barley, wheat or oats, the grain will weigh 1 avoirdupois pound.[5] This is startling enough, but the recognition that the avoirdupois pound was part of the Megalithic system of measurement led to another realization. We came to recognize that the Megalithic system of measurement was not simply based on the size of the Earth, but also on the mass of the Earth.

In the Megalithic system the passage of time and geometry were measured in exactly same way. For example, unlike modern geometry, 1 Megalithic minute of the Earth's circumference is the same thing as 1 Megalithic minute of time. It is a totally integrated system that deals with geometry, time, distance, mass and volume. As a result it can be said to be more advanced than even the metric system we use today. This is because in our modern world the measurement of time is completely divorced from other measurements, whereas in the Megalithic system everything responded to the same logic and the same numbers.

When we saw the whole system in its wonderful simplicity we came to realize that we *must* be correct in our assumptions and in the way we had interpreted the evidence. If not, we had invented the most incredible measuring system imaginable and one that is infinitely more advanced than the systems we presently use. Chris and I are both adamant that we are simply not that clever.

The reader can imagine that our discoveries, or rather rediscoveries, have not been any more popular with orthodox archaeologists and scientists than was Thom's Megalithic Yard. We have some sympathy with them. How could it possibly be that people living in the Stone Age and the Bronze Age could have possessed the information necessary to create such a system? It is true that these people were no less intelligent than we are, but they did not have access to the same technology we enjoy. It would have been extremely difficult for them to assess the polar circumference of the Earth to the level of accuracy indicated by the Megalithic system, and there is no way they could possibly have known the Earth's mass, which was not accurately established until the late 18th century.

An integrated system such as this, based on both the circumference and the mass of the Earth, is surprisingly easy to understand and use but fiercely difficult to create. As we will come to see, when one considers the way this also has a bearing on the Sun and the Moon, the task becomes almost unbelievable in its complexity.

What really sets this system apart is its ability to measure everything and yet it never splits a number. In Megalithic geometry and Megalithic measurements generally, there are no fractions or decimal points. It is also all-encompassing. Almost every week, even years after our original discoveries, we still find new ways in which the Megalithic system could have been used. An example of this is something that occurred to me very recently. We live on a planet that has a fairly dense atmosphere. Since even air has a weight, we are subject to atmospheric pressure, which is the weight of the atmosphere bearing down on us. Atmospheric pressure is quite high. It differs from place to place but there is an average, which in imperial terms is 14.7lb per square inch. This is not a particularly easy number to deal with but if we look at the same figures in the Megalithic system we discover that the average atmospheric pressure equals a round 12lb per square Megalithic Inch.

No accurate measuring system devised by humanity is organic – in other words it can never be a totally natural thing. In the past, units of length across the world have been based on the length of a human forearm, the length of a human foot, or on the distance from a king's nose to his outstretched fingers, but all are artificial and, of course, immensely variable. This doesn't really matter as long as everyone in a particular society is singing from the same hymn sheet. In most cultures that have devised measuring systems, standard weights, vessels for capacity and standard lengths preserved in metal have been kept safe, so that units can always be compared and will not vary. In advanced societies such standards are extremely important.

Measurement is the language of society and especially the marketplace. In a complex culture in which, for example, different components of the same machine are made in various locations, it is absolutely essential that everyone is using the same system of measurement. Without measurements we would not know the time of day, could never ascertain if we were getting value for money when we buy our groceries, could not make anything that relied on a pattern, and would be stumped when it came to filling our cars with fuel. Not that there would be any cars because scientists and engineers rely entirely on measuring systems all the time. In short, any society that does not have established measuring systems is going to be somewhat primitive in a technological sense.

Across the vast period of time that humanity has been advancing, many different civilizations used a variety of alternative measurements, but all were 'superimposed' on the world and not drawn from it. The only natural measurements we see around us are the periods of day and night, the changing seasons of the year, and the length of the year itself. Alas, these are not entirely helpful in a day-to-day sense. Day length and night length vary throughout the year, seasons merge into each other, whilst the Earth year does not resolve to an even number of days. The Earth's journey around the Sun takes 365.2564 days, which is not especially helpful to people who haven't yet invented the decimal point.

Ingenious solutions were found for regulating the length of the year and thereby keeping track of it – which is essential to farming communities that rely on planting at the correct time. If the real length of the year is not known and is simply rounded up or down to, say, 365 days, things will eventually go wrong and after a few centuries the hottest days will be appearing in the months that used to be winter. Calendars have been regulated in all manner of ways, often by adding an extra month every now and again, to keep things working smoothly.

In the case of the Megalithic system, everything relies on the number 366. Using the information derived from the Phaistos Disc it was possible to ascertain that the Minoans kept two calendars. One was composed of 366 days, whereas the other resolved to 492 days. After every 492 days, 1 day was removed from the ritual 366 day calendar. This would have kept everything running right for a staggering 10,000 years without any other correction needed – certainly as long as any civilization was likely to last. It is mind-blowing to realize that if we had continued to use the same calendar as the Minoans, and also almost certainly the Megalithic peoples of the far West of Europe, we would still not be even half a day wrong with the true solar year, even after 5,000 years! No other calendar system I have ever studied was so simple and yet so accurate.

There is more to the Megalithic system than we have so far uncovered. A good example came via one of our readers, who ultimately became a fellow researcher. He made a monumental observation regarding temperature. Like all other forms of measurement, temperature is merely a human-devised scale that allows for consistency. In the Celsius system the point at which water freezes is considered to be 0°C and the boiling point of water is 100°C. It works very well but humanity has learned a lot more since the invention of this particular system. We now know about absolute zero, which is the lowest temperature possible – anywhere in the universe.

Seen in terms of the Celsius scale absolute zero occurs at -273.15°C, whilst on the alternative Fahrenheit scale it is -459.67°F. However, if an alternative Megalithic temperature scale is considered, things turn out much tidier and seem to bear absolute zero in mind. If we were to imagine the freezing point of water to be 0° Megalithic and the boiling point of water to be 366° Megalithic, this means that the temperature of absolute zero would be a staggeringly accurate -1,000° Megalithic.[6]

Taken together with everything else we have learned about the Megalithic system, this result is hardly likely to be a coincidence. This being the case it becomes quite obvious that the whole system could never have been dreamed up by a Stone-Age culture living over 5,000 years ago. All the same, anyone with a calculator and a little time to spare can work out all our figures for themselves. The Megalithic system in all its component parts is quite real, but to have devised it from scratch would have been the nightmare to beat all nightmares. Yet it is not a system that could have *developed* gradually and has all the hallmarks of being deliberately devised, with all its components intact from the start.

Following on from our initial findings regarding the Megalithic Yard we were able to study monuments left on the landscape at least 1,000 years older than those Alexander Thom had surveyed. We turned our attention to structures known as 'henges'. Circular in shape, henges are defined by a ditch and bank, and all have at least one entrance. They occur all over the British Isles and some are immense in size. Nobody knows for certain what henges were used for, but it seems to us that they were the obvious precursors to stone circles. Indeed some stone circles, such as Stonehenge in southern England, were built upon earlier henges.

Henges may have been experimental observatories, in which wooden stakes were used instead of stones, so that they could be easily moved to new locations around the circle when necessary. Many of the henges we carefully measured turned out to be built in units of 366 Megalithic Yards or 366 Megalithic Rods, which we took as proof positive that Thom had been correct regarding the Megalithic Yard. This would push knowledge of the Megalithic system back to at least 3500BC, when many of the henges were constructed.

However, those who created the henges and then the later standing stone circles did not need to know *everything* about the Megalithic system of measurement. Rather they only needed to understand those parts of it that related to their own endeavours.

If I was to go back in time now, in order to teach the Megalithic builders everything they needed to know about the system – in other words the parts of it that were essential to their requirements and to the constructions they left – the task would not be a difficult one. For example, they did not need to know the true astronomical implications of the Megalithic Yard – merely how to recreate it using a pendulum, a few wooden stakes and an observation of the planet Venus. If it was made plain to the people concerned that this procedure was something 'holy' and direct from the gods, it would certainly have been remembered and used. It would not take much in the way of a few simple tricks using modern technology to convince anyone living in that distant era that I was of a supernatural origin.

Message in a Bottle

The Megalithic system in its totality is the best evidence of a 'message in a bottle' that has been left for us, and which, it seems to me, was deliberately created to serve this very purpose. Sooner or later someone, or more likely a succession of people, were going to trip over the components of the Megalithic system of measurements and would fit the pieces together as we did. They must ultimately be forced to the conclusion that a very advanced culture had 'fed' components of the system into societies at an extremely early date. However, this is a very strange sort of message because it is as if further messages were placed in the same bottle but at different times.

We are aware that both the pound and the pint are derived from the Megalithic Yard but these are both units for which the late Stone-Age and Bronze-Age people of Western Europe could have had no real use. Both units rely on an accurate cube being made, which must have sides of exactly 1/10th of a Megalithic Yard (4 Megalithic Inches). To construct such a cube would have been extremely difficult at such a remote date. Chris did manage to make one from clay, but it was made from the sort of clay that does not need to be fired. Real clay shrinks when fired and a significant amount of trial and error would have been necessary in order to create a truly accurate example. In any case, examples of the pound and the pint do not occur in the historical record until at least the 12th century of the modern era. Both were common throughout Europe but varied from place to place. The pint that relates to the Megalithic Yard is the imperial pint.

In the United States the standard pint still used is somewhat smaller than the imperial pint. As the name implies, the imperial pint relates to the British Empire. American colonies were formed and also split away from Britain some time *before* imperial measurements were standardized. The form of pint still used in the US is the same as that which the first settlers took with them as early as the 16th century. This is not especially surprising. Versions of both the pint and the pound were used across a wide geographical area and varied considerably from place to place.

Imperial measurements were standardized in 1824 under the British Weights and Measures Act and it was decided at this time, which size of pint, pound and other measurements should be the standard in Britain and across its Empire. At this time a gallon was defined as being equal to 10 imperial pounds of distilled water at 62°F and a pint was 1/8th of the resulting liquid. As a result the imperial pint weighed 1.25lb.

Of course the pint was ultimately tied to the imperial pound, which derived from an earlier unit known as the avoirdupois pound. This had been created by London merchants in 1303, but ultimately owed its existence to international trade fairs that were held in Champagne, France, from the 12th century. Champagne, in turn, had borrowed the pound from the ancient Romans. They had used a unit which they called 'the libra', which is why the letters lb are still used as shorthand to identify the pound of mass, and to distinguish it from the pound as used for British currency. However, the Roman libra was significantly lighter than the imperial pound.

As for the standard British pound – that had existed as a genuine weight, made in Elizabethan times in the 16th century and kept in the Palace of Westminster. It was originally kept at the Tower of London and so was known as a Tower pound. It was lost when the Palace of Westminster was destroyed by a fire in 1834. A new pound weight was created from platinum but there is no certainty what this was based on because the original standard weight had been destroyed. It is therefore fair to say that the *absolute* imperial pound was not defined until after 1834. It is this standard from which the imperial pint was set.

So we can see that the pound and pint, which fit so neatly into the Megalithic system, both being obtained from a cube with sides of exactly 1/10th of a Megalithic Yard, probably did not even exist in their exact form prior to 1834. All the same, both units – the pint defined by the volume of water held by the cube, and the pound by the weight of cereal grain that would fill the cube – had already existed theoretically since the Megalithic Yard was first used as early as 3500BC. Of course, it might be suggested that we are looking at a bizarre coincidence, but if so it is truly odd. This is because a cube with sides of 1 Megalithic Yard would hold exactly 1,000 pints, and the weight of cereal grain in such a cube would be exactly 1,000lb! Such a result is hard to imagine as a random chance event.[7] What is more, it can be shown that the imperial pound is much more than a Megalithic unit – it is also tied inextricably to the mass of the Earth itself.

It would take interventions at different stages on the timeline to offer the whole Megalithic system. To those who used the system first, only the standard units of length were necessary. They did not need to know, and in fact could never have known, that the Megalithic Yard was derived from the exact polar circumference of the Earth. This fact and others, although inherent in the system, were not monitored by anyone throughout history until our own research began 20 years ago. The earliest people involved were also supplied with the 366-day year and the rectification necessary to keep it in line with the true solar year.

It was absolutely necessary for the Megalithic Yard to be used in the very first structures created by the late Stone-Age people of the British Isles. The measurement had to be there so that Alexander Thom could find it. Similarly, it had to have been used, in its geometric form, in the very earliest of the structures created in the British Isles, namely henges. There it appears as units of 366 Megalithic Yards, which is 1 Megalithic second of the Earth's polar circumference, and so proves the unique geometry involved.

As we will presently see, the Megalithic system goes much further than the confines of the Earth, though once again these facts did not need to be known until our own more recent research highlighted them. Nevertheless, all parts of the Megalithic system had to be in place right at the start of the adventure, whether they were needed at that time or not, and the only way this could have been achieved is with the benefit of hindsight.

As far as the Megalithic system as a whole is concerned, it now becomes obvious that the interventions that took place were something like the following. This may be a simplified version of the events but it serves to commence a timeline for the necessary interventions:

Circa 3500BC: The pre-Megalithic cultures of the British Isles were shown how to create and use the Megalithic Yard, both singly and in its Earth geometrical form of 366 Megalithic Yards. These were incorporated into the henges – the experimental naked-eye observatories that can still be found across the British landscape – and also into the later stone circles and alignments.

Circa 2000BC: The developing Minoan culture on the Island of Crete had to be introduced to its own unit of linear measurement, the Minoan Foot. The Minoans also had to be introduced to the ingenious and incredibly accurate method for regulating the calendar – as demonstrated by the number systems inherent in the Phaistos Disc.

Circa AD1150: Influence had to be placed upon those organizing the Champagne fairs that took place in France and which attracted merchants from all over the known world. It was at these gatherings that the pound of weight first appeared, most specifically in the city of Troyes, Champagne.

Circa AD1560: Action was most likely taken to make certain that the Elizabethan Tower pound unit closely approximated what would later be the imperial pound.

Circa AD1834: When a fire destroyed the Palace of Westminster it was undoubtedly necessary to intervene and to make certain that the new standard unit for the imperial pound was exactly what it turned out to be.

1945–85: Alexander Thom embarked on and continued his careful surveying of Megalithic structures in Britain and France, thereby rediscovering the Megalithic Yard. (This may not have been an intervention but a natural occurrence.)

1995 onward: Alan Butler and Christopher Knight took up the baton on behalf of the late Alexander Thom, thereby gradually uncovering the whole Megalithic system. (This, too, may not have been an intervention but a natural occurrence.)

2000 onward: Alan Butler and Chris Knight made the most revolutionary discoveries regarding the Megalithic system as it relates to both the Moon and the Sun. (This, too, may not have been an intervention but a normal occurrence.)

Our research was not restricted to the Megalithic system of measurements because we also found ourselves drawn into the very peculiar circumstances surrounding barley seeds, Sumerian measures and the eventual creation of the Metric system. Within these apparently unrelated events lie another series of interventions.

CHAPTER 9

Measure for Measure (2)

T he people referred to as the Sumerians inhabited the region that is today known as Iraq. They created a number of city-states between the rivers Tigress and Euphrates, in a geographical area that is often known as the Fertile Crescent. Where the Sumerians originally came from remains something of a mystery, but what is not in doubt is the tremendous bearing their culture would have on humanity, right up to the present day.

Sumerian civilization began to appear as long ago as 4000BC, when what must once have been groups of small agricultural villages began to grow together to form the first co-operative city-states. These earliest Sumerians are recognized for their ability to work together in order to grow vast amounts of grain and other plant crops, and to create large herds of cattle and sheep. This allowed an increase in population and also led to a high degree of specialization, and sufficient wealth for a strong ruling elite with extensive bureaucratic support structures to develop. Most of our present knowledge of the Sumerians comes from the vast number of clay tablets they left behind, which are replete with cuneiform writing and are devoted to all manner of subjects, all the way from religion and mythology to accounts for grain distribution.

We owe a great deal to the Sumerians. Amongst other things, they were the first culture to develop writing; they invented the wheel and soon became adept astronomers and mathematicians. The Sumerians were the first people to measure time in more or less the same way we still do and they were also responsible for the first use of geometry of the 360° type.

The in-depth research Chris Knight and I undertook into the Sumerians for our book *Civilization One* allowed me to explore something that had puzzled me for most of my adult life. I had always wondered where modern geometry had originated. Since in geometry, circles are composed of 360°, I reasoned that its development must have had something to do with the Earth year. The Sumerians kept a fairly accurate calendar that was based on 360 days to the year, so the connection seemed obvious. Of course, the Earth year is not 360 days, but the Sumerians dealt with this problem by adding an extra month to the calendar whenever it was needed, rather than using a 365-day year and leap years as we do today.

What I eventually discovered was that geometry of the 360° variety was indeed associated with the Earth year, but it was actually a lunar construct. In a ritual sense and for administrative purposes, the Sumerians split their year into months, which were tied to the phases of the Moon. To pass from full Moon, through new Moon and back to full Moon again takes 29.53 days. Ancient peoples did not like splitting numbers, so the Sumerian scribes considered the lunar phase period to be 30 days in length. Meanwhile they also chose to split the day and night into 12 units, which we would call hours. (Hours were doubled in the period after the Sumerians so that there were eventually 24 hours in a day.)

The 360° in geometry represent all of the hours in a 30-day month, because 30 x 12 = 360. In the minds of the Sumerian priests and scribes the Moon passed around the Earth in 30 days in a great circle. Each hour that passed on the Earth represented 1° of the Moon's path on that journey. In reality this was a great over-simplification of the way the Moon behaves for several reasons, but that did not really matter because the system worked well for the Sumerians and it became the basis of the way geometry works. A minute of arc of the Moon's hypothetical journey was equal to a minute of time on the Earth, and 1 second of arc equated to 1 second of time.

Sumer was the first large, urban civilization (though ancient Egypt developed at around the same time). The whole culture was dependent on trade, particularly with regard to food. Not everyone in Sumerian civilization was a farmer. Specialists, such as priests, scribes, smiths, builders and the like, still needed to be fed and it was the surplus created by efficient farming that allowed this to happen. Good markets depend on accurate measuring systems and the Sumerians certainly had these. Despite howls of protest from some experts today, it is quite obvious that underpinning the measuring system of all the Sumerian city-states was a linear unit, upon which everything else was originally based.[8] This unit was called the kush, which is also known as the barley cubit. It was most commonly found in its double form, and for good reason. Since the Sumerians became great bureaucrats and had a written language, they have left us ample evidence of how this linear unit came about. The double kush was equal to 360 barley seeds. Modern experts suggest that the barley seed mentioned in Sumerian texts was nothing more than a 'ritualized' seed. The reason for this is probably because someone in the recent past assumed that no accurate unit of linear measure could be established by something as apparently haphazard as barley seeds.

If 360 barley seeds are laid end to end, the resultant length is much greater than the double kush. We know how long the double kush was because of sample measures that have been found by archaeologists, most notably on some statues of the Sumerian king, Gudea, who reigned around 2140BC. Using the measure shown on the statues it is possible to ascertain a length of 49.94cm for the kush and therefore 99.88cm for the double kush; in other words, incredibly close to a modern metre.

Barley grains and wheat grains were once also used in old British and European measures, but these eventually become stylized and no longer related to the plant crop. This is probably another reason why it is assumed that the same was true in Sumer, but this was not the case. When I took 360 modern barley seeds and laid them side by side and on their sides[9], rather than end to end, I discovered that the Sumerians were telling the absolute truth because even 360 modern barley seeds, when placed in this way, do indeed measure around 99.88cm. I undertook this experiment several times, using a mixture of both small and larger seeds, and on average the result was very accurate.

But this was not the only way to define the length of the double kush. A very similar process to that adopted by the Megalithic priests could have been and almost certainly was used. As in the Megalithic case, Venus as an evening star was observed. In this case the gap the planet traversed was not 1 Megalithic degree of the horizon but rather 1 modern degree. As in the Megalithic model (explained in Appendix 1) a braced wooden frame would have been employed to track Venus, and a pendulum was used. Rather than swinging 366 times, the Sumerian pendulum was observed to swing 240 times during Venus's progression across 1 degree of the sky. This is because there are 240 seconds of time in 1 degree of Venus travel, which takes slightly over 4 modern minutes. A pendulum that swings back or forth 240 times during this period, and at the latitude of Sumer, will measure 99.88cm. Thus there are two different ways of accurately assessing the length of a Sumerian double kush.

From a mythological perspective there is evidence of an association between the planet Venus and measurement in Sumerian culture. The Sumerians had many gods and goddesses, but none was more important than Inanna. She was, at one and the same time, the goddess of both love and war; in most respects a character of extremes, primarily because of a dualistic nature born of her astronomical association. Inanna was the godly personification of the planet Venus and her duality represented the alternate morning-star and evening-star appearances of the planet. No other deity inspired more reverence in Sumer. A high priestess, who always ruled as Inanna's earthly representative, seems to have had a rank and station equal to that of a king.

There is no doubt about the association of Inanna with the planet Venus because the Sumerians were explicit about the fact. Her main emblem was an eight-pointed star, which is appropriate for Venus. This is because the Earth and Venus have related orbital periods in which, when seen from the Earth, five Venus cycles is equal to eight Earth years. Epic poems were written about Inanna, who to the later Babylonians was known as Ishtar. In one of these poems Inanna travels to the underworld, but unlike any other individual she is eventually allowed to return to the world of the living. In order to enter the underworld Inanna has to gradually remove all her clothes and jewellery. This may relate to the fact that Venus, like the Moon, undergoes 'phases' – in other words we do not see the full light of Venus all the time. Like the Earth, Venus is a planet and the part of it we see at any point in time is determined by its relationship with the Sun.

Inanna's journey to the underworld is undoubtedly a mythological explanation for the behaviour of Venus as seen from Earth. Venus can be seen as either a morning star, appearing before dawn, or an evening star, following the Sun as it sets in the evening, dependent on the Earth's own orbit relative to that of Venus. To the ancients generally, events that took place at night were associated with the underworld – the domain of sleep and death – so it is possible that Inanna was considered to be 'in' the underworld when Venus was in the evening-star part of its orbit. In the myth of Inanna travelling to the underworld, the poem tells us that she dressed herself very carefully, and that she made certain that she carried the correct items. In translation the poem says:

> She placed a golden ring on her hand. She held the lapis-lazuli measuring rod and measuring line in her hand.

The lapis-lazuli measuring rod was undoubtedly a 'sample' linear unit, such as the ones that are still held in all countries. These days they are usually made of some very precious metal, such as platinum. The Sumerians undoubtedly used lapis-lazuli because it was at one and the same time the most beautiful and precious stone they possessed. The measuring line might well relate to the pendulum that was used in conjunction with the movements of Venus to set, and then periodically check, the length of the sample rod.

On her journey to the underworld Inanna had to pass a number of different gates. It is at each of these in turn that she was divested of some of her possessions and clothing. There were seven gates in all, and it was not until the sixth gate that Inanna had to give up the measuring rod and measuring line.

After Venus crosses the Sun in its transition from a morning star to an evening star, it moves very quickly along the path of the zodiac. Of course this is a line-of-sight effect caused by not only the orbit of Venus but that of the Earth, which is also travelling around the Sun. It is during this period, as Venus grows further and further from the Sun as an evening star, that the pendulum experiment necessary to set the double kush can be carried out. It takes Venus around 280 days to get as far away from the Sun as it can when an evening star, but as it nears the end of its elongation from the Sun, its movement within the zodiac slows, until eventually it stops altogether and then begins to move in the opposite direction – gradually dropping back towards the Sun.

For most of its journey away from the Sun as an evening star, Venus is travelling within the zodiac by 1°14' per day but it is during the last 40 days or so it slows significantly. This coincides very well with the fact that Inanna had to give up her measuring rod and measuring line at the sixth gate of the underworld because Venus moves away from the Sun for 7 x 40 days. It is around 6 x 40 days that it apparently slows within the zodiac, meaning that if the experiment was attempted the pendulum would deliver a shorter measure.

It looks as though the story of Inanna entering the underworld contains genuine astronomical information that would have been of use to the Sumerian astronomer priests. What a wonderful metaphor and instruction this is, and it only goes to prove that there are often hidden messages in mythological stories.

Once again we find cries of protest coming from experts when the suggestion is made that all other units of Sumerian measurement were based on the length of the double kush, but as with the barley seeds, it is obvious that this was indeed the case. A cube with sides 1/10th of a double kush holds almost exactly a litre of water, and of course the weight of the water in such a cube is almost exactly 1kg. To the Sumerians these were the units they called respectively the sila and the double mana. Astonishingly, as with the linear unit, the Sumerian unit of weight could also be defined in terms of barley seeds. The Sumerians stated that the weight of 360 x 60 barley seeds defined 1 double mana. When I weighed modern barley seeds I discovered that this is still the case and to a great degree of accuracy. In other words the weight of 360 x 60 barley seeds and the weight of water held in a cube with sides of 1/10th of a double kush are the same.

As time went by and the civilization matured, a frightening array of weights and measures began to appear in the various city-states, but what is obvious is that the closer one gets to the foundation of Sumer, the more accurately defined the various units of measurement are. Clearly the system did not improve with the passing of time – rather it became somewhat muddled. One gets the impression that, like the Megalithic system, it began with a strict series of instructions.

It is important to recognize just how unlikely and therefore significant this series of rediscoveries is. The fact that the Sumerian double kush could be defined by means of a Venus pendulum strengthens the evidence that the Megalithic peoples used the same technique. Undoubtedly the procedure was in the hands of the elite. Not everyone in Sumerian society would have had the knowledge necessary to undertake the task, but in such a structured society sample measures and weights could be and were produced.

What probably worries modern experts, and especially scientists, is that the Sumerian system of weights and measures so closely resembles the modern metric system. The metric system did not appear until the late 18th century, in France. At this period, Europe's systems of measurement were in a shocking state of disarray, which meant international trade was extremely complicated and subject to mistakes. Members of the French Academy of

Science were tasked with finding a new system of measures that would be easy to use and which could be universally applied. The scientists were only too happy to oblige because developing scientific endeavour also relied on accurate and consistent measurements.

Their original idea was to base the system on the length of a seconds pendulum (a pendulum that swings back or forth during one second of time). The seconds pendulum had been understood for some decades. A pendulum was seen as being truly scientific because the only things that have a bearing on the timing of a pendulum swing are the force of gravity, which varies very little from place to place, and the length of the string. If the latitude at which pendulum experiments were carried out was prescribed, then no variables remained and it could become an invaluable aid to establishing an accurate unit of length on which everything else could be based.

The English all-round genius Isaac Newton (1643–1727) had experimented with the seconds pendulum at a latitude of 45° and declared it to be equal to 440.428 lignes, which in modern terms is 99.535cm. There is no absolutely clear evidence as to why the seconds pendulum length was not used for the new French system but it probably came down to two facts.

1 At the end of the 18th century, clocks were only just becoming really accurate and the most precise examples available were probably not those in France at the time. To create an accurate and unchanging seconds pendulum, one obviously needed a very true clock. It could be that the members of the French Academy of Science doubted that they could establish enough consistency between clocks to recreate the chosen unit of length if it was lost. It does not seem to have occurred to them to use an astronomical method.

2 At this time the French had embarked on an experiment to measure the Earth. They intended to establish the length of a

quadrant running from the North Pole to the Equator, through France. With a mixture of pride in their own abilities and a desire to be as accurate as possible in the creation of the new unit of linear length, an Earth measurement was proposed.

The linear unit chosen for the new measuring system was equal to a ten-millionth part of the distance between the North Pole and the Equator. This was called the metre. All the other measurements in the metric system, which as its name implies was a base-ten system, were derived from the metre, or its 1/100th division, the centimetre. For example, the water held in a cube with sides of 10cm was considered to be a litre, and the weight of that water was a kilogram.

So similar is the French metric system to the Sumerian model that we wondered at first whether someone in France at the end of the 18th century *knew* how the Sumerians had handled measurements, but this cannot be the case (except by way of intervention). At the time the metric system was devised, very little in the way of archaeology had taken place in Sumer. In any case, most of what we know about the Sumerians comes courtesy of the many thousands of clay tablets impressed with cuneiform writing that they left behind. The struggle to understand written Sumerian still goes on and had not even begun when the metric system was devised.

In my opinion this whole scenario demonstrates a classic example of intervention at work. If the French had indeed based the metric system on the length of a true seconds pendulum, it would *not* have looked as similar to the Sumerian system as it does. This is because the length of the true seconds pendulum at 45° latitude is around 99.5cm, whereas the Venus-derived pendulum is longer, closely approaching a modern metre. A metre derived from the Earth's quadrant is of course 100cm and so is incredibly close to the Venus-derived pendulum length, which is 99.88cm.

What history has left to us are two entire systems of measurement, the Sumerian system and the metric system, divided by around 4,000 years but as good as identical in their construction. There is an observation in science that suggests nature will invariably answer the same problems in the same way. As just one example, across millions of years fossil evidence shows there have been a number of animals that are referred to as 'sabre-toothed tigers', though in reality many of these creatures were not directly related to each other and were divided by great stretches of time. This happened because nature was faced with a set of requirements for a successful mammalian predator and natural selection came up with a very similar answer. However, this cannot explain the similarity between the Sumerian measuring system and the metric system. It is true that the starting point in each case was a useable, integrated way of measuring things, but the basic unit in each case was derived in an entirely different way; and yet it is all but identical.

As with other points of intervention we are *meant* to take notice, and the fact that I contributed to the book *Civilization One* and am now compiling this particular chapter proves that this is exactly what has happened. The very similarity of the two systems of measurement caused us to look much more closely at the Sumerians than we might otherwise have done, and in particular at the basis of the Sumerian measures – the barley seed.

Barley is an extremely useful plant. It is part of the grass family and is derived from the wild *Hordeum vulgare*. Barley was one of the first and most probably *the* first species of plant that was deliberately tamed for human use and production. Wild barley isn't so different from its modern counterpart except in one important respect. Wild barley has a brittle stalk, especially the spikelet that supports the grains. When the barley grain is mature, this spikelet shatters and the seeds in the head of the barley are automatically dispersed. Domestic barley spikes do not shatter in the same way, which means the seeds are retained in the ear until they are separated by threshing after harvest.

The earliest archaeological finds of wild barley that may have been part of the human hunter-gatherer larder are from close to the Sea of Galilee in the Middle East. These examples have been dated to around 8500BC, and some experts suggest that domesticated barley may extend back as far as 6,800 years or even longer. There are two distinct forms of cultivated barley, which are known respectively as 'two-row' and 'six-row'. Two-row barley is likely to have been the first to be domesticated. In this variety the ear has three spikelets alternating along the rachis or central spike. Only the central spikelet carries seeds, whilst the other two remain infertile. In the case of six-row barley, all three spikelets bear seeds. Both types of barley are still grown because two-row barley has a lower content of protein than six-row barley. This makes two-row barley better for brewing beer because it has a greater sugar content that can be given over to fermentation. Both forms of barley have been used for making bread, and barley is also an ideal animal feed.

It could be that barley is the most useful plant humanity has ever possessed. It is extremely adaptable in that it can grow in very temperate and even relatively cold climates, such as Scandinavia; yet at the same time it is very tolerant of dry conditions and can also thrive in near-desert areas. As I have already suggested, barley is extremely important when it comes to making beer and, quite apart from its ability to get people tipsy, beer has been one of the saving graces of mankind. The brewing of beer involves a vigorous boiling of the water involved and this ensures that all germs present in that water will be killed. Since the purity of water supplies, especially in hot climates, cannot be guaranteed, the consumption of beer on a large scale may have saved countless thousands of lives. In Western Europe during the medieval period, beer was drunk by everyone, even children, with men drinking up to a gallon each day. People who drank *only* beer were much less likely to contract deadly infections, such as cholera, than those who consumed water.

So important (even crucial) was barley to ancient cultures such as the Sumerians and the Egyptians that both cultures had powerful and well-served deities that were responsive to this one food plant. As a result it might not seem too strange that barley was used as the basis of a measuring system – as indeed was originally the case in cultures other than the Sumerians. All the same, this is only part of the story.

We knew that the Sumerian double mana, based on a double kush of 99.88cm, weighed 0.996kg. We were also very much aware that the Megalithic system of measurement had been based not only on the circumference of the Earth but also on its mass, and we wondered if the same had been true with regard to Sumerian measures. What a shock we were in for when we looked!

In Ian Nicholson's faithful book *Astronomy – A Dictionary of Space and the Universe*[10] the mass of the Earth is quoted as being 5.976×10^{24} kilograms. However, if we were to turn these measurements into Sumerian double mana, by dividing by 0.996, *the result is an exact and perfectly round 6×10^{24} double mana*. This is surprising enough, but not half so stunning as when one realizes that the Sumerians used a sexagesimal or base-60 system of counting!

What this means is that if we were to segment the Earth like an orange, and take a segment that was equal to 1° of arc of the Earth's circumference, its mass would be equal to that of 100,000,000,000,000,000,000,000 barley seeds.

Could such a situation have come about by chance? I think most readers will agree with me when I suggest that such an eventuality is so unlikely that, at some level or another, we have to see an *intention* here. So how could this have been brought about?

One of the most surprising realizations springing from all the experiments I carried out with barley seeds was how very little they had changed in the several thousand years since they were grown in Sumer. The seeds I used, which were of two-row barley from an organic crop grown in England, proved to be identical in size and weight to those upon which the Sumerian system had been based. What is more, when I checked my figures for weight against those of previous British crops from decades ago, the results were always consistent.

Nobody denies that barley has been one of the greatest friends humanity has had since the days of farming began, but it may not have been there at all by chance. All that would be required for things to turn out exactly as they did, would be for our future selves to take seed, from present wild and possibly also domesticated barley, back in time to well before humanity sought to live a settled life. The plant, which grows prolifically almost anywhere, would flourish and prosper until such times as it was needed by humanity as it sought to establish a farming existence. When the Sumerians were ready to create an integrated measuring system using the barley seeds, they would be bound to lock into the results shown above – though, of course, they need not have had the slightest clue that this was the case.

The progress of our world in a modern sense has been totally dependent on farming. As far as I can establish, no civilization worth the title has ever sprung from nomadic people or from hunter-gatherers. There have been some ostensible exceptions, for example that of the Mongols, who conquered large parts of Central Asia and Eastern Europe. However, the Mongols, though nomadic in a historical sense, were able to build their empire because they were benefiting from the agricultural lifestyle of the people they conquered. In the main, those civilizations upon which human advancement depended were all reliant on a settled lifestyle made possible by farming.

The writer Jared Diamond, who is a professor of geography and psychology at the University of Los Angeles wrote an excellent book in 1997 entitled *Guns, Germs and Steel*. Diamond sought to demonstrate why Europe, and particularly Western Europe, eventually came to control so much of the planet. He sees many factors being involved but, like me, he stresses the importance of a stable, ordered agricultural community. The so-called cradle of civilization did not lie in Western Europe, but rather in the Middle East and Diamond demonstrates how Western Europe became the beneficiary of the advances made further east. In doing so he places much emphasis on cereal crops, and particularly barley. Nowhere was the connection between barley and the development of a settled life, with the luxury of specialists who could furnish a technological revolution, more obvious than in Sumer. It is thanks to intensive, successful agriculture and animal domestication that the Sumerians developed writing, mathematics, geometry, calendars, technological innovations such as the wheel, and so much else for which later cultures had the people of the Fertile Crescent to thank.

The burning question is – did all this come about by chance, or was there a series of direct, planned interventions that allowed people living in the right geographical and climatic circumstances to start ploughing the land and to ultimately build the first cities?

In the light of natural, human ingenuity it might seem totally unnecessary to postulate a situation in which early cultures were *encouraged* and *helped* to develop farming, urban life, measuring systems and the like. However, the idea that all of this took place purely as a result of random chance events allied to developing human capabilities does not take account of the fact that, in the case of the measuring systems, we find them appearing little by little, across vast periods of time. Despite this, in the case of both the Megalithic system and the Sumerian/metric system, the full scope and ingenuity of the final systems had to be in place from the start.

One example will probably suffice here. We have seen that it is possible to set the length of both the Megalithic Yard and the Sumerian double kush/metre, by using a pendulum and the movements of the planet Venus. Both the Megalithic Yard and the Sumerian double kush have a significance far beyond being simple, culturally accepted standard units of measure. But how could either the Stone-Age people of the far west of Europe or the first settlers in Sumer have known this? The Megalithic Yard is a geodetic unit, tied to a system of geometry that, as we shall see, is not only specifically applicable to the Earth but also to the Moon and the Sun. As bright as the people who planned and erected structures such as Stonehenge in southern England may have been, logic asserts that they could not have known about the *absolute* size of the Earth, let alone that of the Moon or the Sun. For them to have devised a standard unit that took all three bodies into account, and which was also directly related to the mass of the Earth by chance is unthinkable.

Similarly, the Sumerians devised a unit of linear measure that was definable not only by using the pendulum and an observation of Venus, but also employing simple barley seeds. Their unit too, as well as the very barley seeds that could be used to define it, was directly and very accurately tied to the mass of the Earth, and in a way that reflects what we know to have been the working matrix of the sexagesimal system they used.

In terms of the movements of Venus, the Megalithic Yard and the double kush, which came first? If a standard unit of linear length was required by any culture, it could be defined in the same way as the Venus method, but using a star – come to that any star! It would be just as accurate as using Venus and, as long as the same methodology was used, it would never vary. If such a unit had been tied to 360° geometry there is a good chance that it would have turned out to be about 47cm, based on swinging the pendulum 360 times during the passage of Venus across 1° of the sky. A unit of this length would have been perfectly adequate for the purposes of the marketplace but it would not have related directly to the dimensions of the Earth, the Moon and the Sun, or to the Earth's mass.

The emergence of the pound, the pint and the gallon as late as the Middle Ages, and the metric system as recently as the late 18th century seems to indicate something much more than random chance in the case of both the Megalithic Yard and the double kush/metre. We are *meant* to take note of these occurrences, and to ask ourselves how and why they could have come about. Both units are tied to the movements of the planet Venus, but have other implications about which their first users could not have known. It is therefore quite obvious to me that in both cases the priest/scribes involved were *told* what to do and *how* to do it.

We must be prepared to adopt the adage of Arthur Conan Doyle through the mouth of his fictitious detective Sherlock Holmes.

> … when you have eliminated the impossible, *whatever* remains, however improbable, must be the truth.

The people of our own future know and understand both the Megalithic system of geometry and measurement, and the true basis of the metric system. That is self-evident because they are both explained in this book and others previously published by Chris Knight and myself. They therefore clearly have what they need to go back in time and to seed both the cultures in question with the relevant information. It is not only desirable for them to do so, it is vital – and since it happened and is part of the history of the world we can assume that they took the responsibility seriously.

Anyone who accepts what we are suggesting about the Megalithic system and the Sumerian system, but who is unwilling to look seriously at intervention theory would have to explain what has happened in some other way. Meanwhile those who will not even look at the facts and who suggest that the Megalithic system, in particular, is a figment of our collective imagination, would have to go on to explain how something that doesn't really exist at all could be so relevant to our part of the solar system and to the developing history of humanity.

CHAPTER 10

A Strange Departure

No sooner had we finished writing our first book together, *Civilization One*, than we found ourselves catapulted into a new area of research. It was one that was totally unexpected and quite bizarre.

To recap – we were aware that the Megalithic Yard, rediscovered by Professor Alexander Thom in his scrupulous measurement of hundreds of Stone-Age and Bronze-Age monuments in Britain, was a geodetic unit. This means that when allied to Megalithic 366-degree geometry, the Megalithic Yard shows itself to fit the polar circumference of the Earth in a logical and obviously intended way. Thus we see that in the polar circumference of the Earth there are 366 Megalithic Yards to 1 Megalithic second of arc; 6 Megalithic seconds to 1 Megalithic minute of arc; 60 Megalithic minutes to 1 Megalithic degree; and 366 Megalithic degrees in the polar circumference of the Earth. What we did not expect was that this most useful of linear units would serve a very similar job for both the Moon and the Sun.

We came upon this realization more or less by chance. In fact exactly how our attention was drawn to it neither of us can now remember. It probably occurred because we were well aware that the Earth is 3.66 times larger than the Moon. This figure stands out because of the constant reoccurrence of the number 366 in the Megalithic system. But what it does mean is that on the Moon each Megalithic second of arc must equal 100 Megalithic Yards. When we took note of accurate measurements of the Moon, this turned out to be the case to a stunning degree of accuracy.

It then did not take long for us to realize that if the Megalithic Yard served this rather remarkable function on the Moon, it *must* do something similar for the Sun. We were well aware that, apparently through some random but convenient reason, our Sun is 400 times larger than Earth's Moon. Why is this important? It is significant because as it orbits the Earth, the Moon is capable of standing exactly 1/400th part of the distance between the Earth and the Moon. This in turn is what leads to the occurrence of perfect solar eclipses, in which the shadow of the Moon covers the face of the Sun and sends parts of the world into temporary darkness.

Putting aside for a moment the fact that perfect solar eclipses are so very, very unlikely, that they occur at all drew us to look more closely at the dimensions of the Sun. Our first assumption was quite correct – 1 Megalithic second of arc on the Moon measures 100 Megalithic Yards; and 1 Megalithic second of arc on the Sun measures 40,000 Megalithic Yards.

If this was a genuine coincidence, it was a strange one indeed, but of course coincidences do happen. Fortunately, we did not leave the situation at that, but rather took a diversion to look more closely at our nearest companion in space, which turns out to be the strangest body imaginable.

Our own research into the Moon happened to turn up at a time when Earth's satellite was beginning to attract all sorts of attention from scientists. They were beginning to realize that this great lump of rock, silently orbiting the Earth every month, was far more important than simply representing a convenient lantern on certain nights. It turns out, and in fact no scientist involved in this research would argue the point now, that without the Moon we would not be here at all. Everything that grows, swims, crawls, flies above or walks on the surface of the Earth does so because of the presence and particular specifications of the Moon. All life on Earth became possible because of the presence of the Moon.

The Earth occupies an area of space relative to the Sun that is known these days as the 'Goldilocks Zone'. As I mentioned earlier in the book, things have to be just right for life to develop – not so cold that water would be perpetually frozen and not so hot that it either only existed as steam or else boiled off and was lost into space. Fortunately for us the Earth orbits the Sun in a very convenient Goldilocks Zone, but it isn't quite as simple as that. Even a young child knows that water on the Earth exists in all three of its states – ice, liquid and gas. This means that the temperatures experienced on Earth allow all three states to be possible, dependent on what part of the planet is getting more or less light and heat from the Sun.

Because of its giant, mostly iron, core, the Earth is actually a very unstable planet. It wobbles significantly on its axis, like a child's spinning top slowing down, and were it not for some external force, it would quite regularly topple over – and probably start spinning in the opposite direction relative to the Sun. Such a state of affairs would be absolutely catastrophic for life. Huge tectonic forces would be generated and if any life were able to withstand the actual event, it would probably be eradicated by the climatic consequences that followed. So, what is it that keeps the Earth's wobble within manageable proportions, and which keeps its attitude with respect to the Sun in a state that is perfect for life to develop and flourish – it is Earth's giant Moon.

The angle of inclination of the Earth as it travels around the Sun is just over 23° and this turns out to be absolutely crucial. This is because such an angle ensures that as the Earth orbits the Sun, different parts of its surface receive greater or lesser amounts of light and heat from the Sun. It is this state of affairs that leads to the Earth's seasons. In summer wherever we happen to live, our part of the Earth is getting more light from the Sun, whereas in winter the Earth is on the other side of the Sun and the opposite hemisphere is getting the lion's share of the light. If this were not the case, some parts of the Earth would receive light and heat all the time, and would eventually become like a furnace, whilst other areas would be so cold that, like the poles, they would be perpetually icebound. As it stands, even the Earth's poles do receive some light and heat – to the extent that the North Pole, which is pure ice and does not cover a continent as the South Pole does, decreases significantly in size each summer.

We all know that the temperature is very hot at the equator, but this heat is nothing compared to what it would be if the Earth's angle of inclination did not ensure an even warming from the Sun.

The Moon has been crucial to the Earth in many other ways. For example, nobody doubts that the material that forms the Moon came from the Earth itself. As we shall see, the absence of this material probably allowed room on the Earth's surface for oceans to form; but more crucially, when it came into existence, the Moon was very much closer to the Earth than it is now, and its gravitational presence never gave the infant Earth a moment's peace. Every time it passed overhead, which was more frequent back then, its huge size and gravitational drag, caused veritable 'tides' to develop in the slowly solidifying rock of the young Earth.

If we look at Earth's two nearest companion planets in the solar system, Venus and Mars, we can see that both are very Earth-like in composition – each is made up of rock and metals. But that is where the similarity ends. Both Venus and Mars have a solid surface – they are not tectonic in the way the Earth is. The Earth's surface is composed of a series of extremely large plates, which float on the underlying magma. It is these tectonic plates that slowly move around the surface of the Earth, carrying with them the continents. The interaction of the tectonic plates is what allows volcanoes and earthquakes to be present. The surface of the Earth is never allowed to settle down and solidify; the reason for this has been, and most likely still is, the presence of so large a companion body as the Moon. True, although Venus has no moons, Mars has two, but these are tiny in comparison with our own Moon and have little or no bearing on their companion planet. Our Moon, on the other hand, is massive, and because it was once so much closer to the Earth than it is now, it has constantly irritated the Earth.

This has been vital because were it not for volcanoes, fresh minerals and metals from the centre of the Earth would not regularly be deposited on its surface. It is the meeting of continents, thanks to the moving tectonic plates, that has thrown up vast mountain ranges as land masses collided. Thanks to our weather systems the mountains gradually 'weather out', once again passing their minerals and metals into rivers and eventually the sea.

The Earth is a very dynamic place, whereas both Venus and Mars are visibly dead, with most of their minerals and metals locked deep below their thick crusts. Both planets have probably undergone significant geological upheavals in the past, but in both cases these seem to have been catastrophic in nature and not the constant, more limited geological processes that take place on the Earth. In the case of Venus it might well have replaced all of its surface rock very recently – which would hardly have been a masterstroke in terms of any life that was developing there.

As the Moon gradually drew away from the Earth and its orbit lengthened, there was an exchange of energy. This had a bearing on the Earth, which was originally spinning much faster than it is right now. As the Earth cooled and liquid water became possible, the Moon was still close enough to ensure that the water was constantly on the move, as it still does today because the majority of tides on our planet come courtesy of the Moon. Early tides were monumental compared to those we experience today. High tides twice every day would have thundered far up early river valleys and across plains, constantly bringing fresh sediment inland, which would one day carry the food upon which early life depended.

Later, when life had developed in the sea, the presence of significant tides encouraged some creatures to eventually wander onto the land, gradually staying there longer and longer until they were no longer dependent on the oceans. And the Moon was still there, to prevent the Earth's crust from solidifying, and through tectonic activity new mountains were formed, weathered out and passed their nutrients to the rivers and oceans.

It is now quite apparent that, without the presence of the Moon, life on Earth would almost certainly never have developed in the first place. And even if it had done so, the chances of it gaining a strong foothold was negligible. We may not have realized it in the past but the Moon is the greatest friend we have.

So, how did the Moon come to be where it is in the first place? If you log onto the internet or pick up a modern text book you will discover that the 'best guess' right now – and make no bones about it, this is a guess – is that a Mars-sized body once collided with the Earth. This sent matter spinning off the surface of the Earth, which eventually coalesced into the Moon. The theory, which is often referred to as the 'big whack' theory, came about because of certain facts regarding the Earth and the Moon. We know from samples of rock brought back from the Moon by astronauts that the com-position of Moon rock is very similar to that of rock found near the surface of the Earth. We also know, because of what are known as oxygen isotopes, that the Earth and the Moon developed in the same part of space – in other words the Moon cannot be a captured asteroid. Finally, Moon rock and Earth rock are of a very similar age – in fact, in most respects they are identical.

The only difference between the Earth and the Moon is that the Moon is much lighter in mass than the Earth. It is 3.66 times smaller than the Earth but has only 1/81st part of Earth's mass. It is therefore obvious that if the Moon was made from the Earth, it wasn't made from the heavy bits of our planet which, because of gravity, lie mainly close to Earth's centre. The big whack theory developed because it was suggested that the impact planet did not completely destroy the Earth – rather, material from closer to Earth's surface was ejected, and this is why the Moon has no heavy metal core.

It's a fine theory as far as it goes, but unfortunately it doesn't go far enough. For example, the oxygen isotope of both Earth rock and Moon rock shows that both developed in the same part of space, but there is no additional oxygen isotope that must have belonged to the rogue planet. There are also problems regarding Earth spin. If we turn back the clock to a period just after Earth had started to cool, which is when theorists suggest the big whack happened, it is possible to project how fast the Earth was spinning. An impact large enough to create the Moon would have had a significant bearing on

Earth's rate of spin, and this is not the case. This caused such a problem with the big whack theory that a second impact, this time from the opposite direction, had to be created as a cause for slowing down the Earth.

For these and other significant reasons, big whack is a best guess, but it may not be the real explanation of the Moon's presence.

The more we looked at the Moon, the weirder things became. Over months of researching we came up with a host of mathematical relationships between the Earth, the Moon and the Sun, which stood out from the background of random chance and which made the Moon into something extremely mysterious. There are many of these relationships, and all of them are high-lighted in our book *Who Built the Moon?*[11], but in the main they rely on three separate series of numbers, which occur all over the place – even in unrelated ways – but which cannot be ignored.

For example, the present orbit of the Moon around the Earth takes 27.322 days; 366 such orbits would equal a very round and unlikely 10,000 days.

As we have seen, the Earth is 3.66 times larger than the Moon in terms of size, which means its size is 27.322 per cent that of the Earth – and of course 27.322 is the number of days in the Moon's orbit around the Earth.

Many of the mathematical puzzles come about because of our choice of the metre and the kilometre as our preferred measurements these days. In other words they exist because of a 'convention' and not because of any naturally occurring phenomena. As an example, I have indicated that the Moon has only 27.322 per cent of Earth's size; it has a circumference of 109.28 kilometres. Not only is this number 4 x 27.322, it is also the ratio of the size of the Earth compared to that of the Sun. Yes! The Sun is 109.28 times larger than the Earth. Of course a ratio such as this has nothing to do with the choice of the kilometre as a preferred measuring unit, but this is only one instance in which the same numbers turn up time and time again with regard to the relationship of the Earth, the Moon and the Sun.

Another number that turns up regularly in this relationship is the number 40 and its multiples. The Moon has a size that is 1/400th part that of the Sun.

It orbits at 1/400th the distance between the Earth and the Sun. In each day the Moon turns 400 kilometres on its axis and in the same day the Earth turns 40,000 kilometres on its axis – a relationship of 100:1. We also find that 40,000 is the number of Megalithic Yards in 1 Megalithic second of arc of the Sun.

In terms of the number 366, we have 366 star days to the Earth year; 366 as the number of Megalithic Yards in 1 Megalithic second of arc of the Earth's polar circumference, as well as this being the number of Megalithic degrees in the Earth's polar circumference. The Moon is 366 per cent smaller than the Earth and, seen another way, the Earth is 3.66 times larger than the Moon.

These repeating series go on and on, appearing in many ways. Not all are directly related because, as I have suggested, those that are relevant to the metric system are literally man-made. But they are present, and our book *Who Built the Moon?* is literally filled with them.

What were we to make of all this? As I suggested a moment ago, coincidences do happen, but when they happen again, and again, and again, to this extent, anyone who possesses a modicum of wisdom is bound to ask what is really going on. The trouble is that the implications of anyone asking this question in terms of the Earth, Moon and Sun relationships is that they are going to find themselves faced with a possible reality that beggars belief.

Nevertheless, truths have to be faced and the truth we looked square in the eye was that all of these number sequences that share the same basic three numbers, could not have appeared by chance. There is every indication of both thought and action involved. To put it bluntly – someone designed the Moon, extrapolating from the already existent relationship of the Earth and the Sun. The Moon was created to be a specific size and mass so that it could do the job for which it had been designed, whilst at the same time co-operating in such a series of quite definite clues that someone must eventually realize what had taken place. It's weird, it's almost beyond belief – but it simply has to be true.

Having eventually realized that we had to think the unthinkable, we then looked again at what lay before us. Most of the messages that the Earth,

Moon and Sun relationships betray are only relevant at this period of time. The Moon was once very much closer to the Earth than it is right now and, as a result, its orbital characteristics would have been very different at that time. Only after around 4 billion years has the Moon adopted its present orbit, which is still gradually lengthening. It is as if whoever or whatever created the Moon was quite well aware of how long it would take something intelligent enough to look up into the sky with wonder to evolve, and so the relevant messages were programmed into the system to appear at that time. And that time is right now!

I suggest that doubting readers take the time out to read *Who Built the Moon?*, which rehearses this argument in a much more complete way than is possible in a single chapter. Incidentally, nobody, not one person out of all those who have bought and read *Who Built the Moon?* has written to tell us why we are wrong in our assumptions or where we have made any mathematical mistake. When scientists, and astronomers in particular, are worried about the implications of a theory that they even half-sense could spell disaster to their careers, they simply tend to ignore it; that's human nature!

Months of discussions and much more research followed as we tried to fathom who or what might have created Earth's moon. We began to realize that the Moon is a machine. True, it's a very large one, but a machine nevertheless; and when one begins to look at things this way, it doesn't sound half as odd to suggest that anyone or anything could be a planet builder.

Our talks ranged across the same ground I rehearsed at the start of this book when I was discussing very early technological achievements that are completely out of kilter with known history. There were also certain facts we had to bear in mind. For starters, many of the 'messages' incorporated into the Earth, Moon and Sun system relate to measuring systems that we have come to know as the Megalithic system, and the metric system, which is actually the Sumerian system in a slightly altered coat. The Moon's creator had to either *know* that these systems would one day exist, or actually participate in their creation, if the messages they had left were to be recognized.

In the end we were forced to the same conclusion that I reached as early as the first chapter of this book. The creatures who had the greatest interest in the Moon being what it is and where it is are us – human beings.

It is true that from the very moment it came into being the Earth was a near perfect Goldilocks planet, but near perfect is nowhere near good enough. For example, the Earth has a very active magnetic field. This exists because of the vast amount of superheated iron that lies at its core. This is as hot as the surface of the Sun but remains solid because of the tremendous pressure exerted on it by the Earth's own gravitational forces. In a way we still do not fully understand, it is this iron core that creates the magnetic field. In turn, the magnetic field of the Earth serves an essential purpose. It reaches out far beyond our planet and diverts most of the harmful radiation that streams out into space from the Sun. Without the magnetic field no life would be possible here and yet the mechanisms that allow the magnetic field to exist make the Earth a very potentially unstable planet. These are the same forces that would see it regularly toppling over, were it not for the stabilizing influence of the Moon.

Neither would the Earth have the tectonic systems, the weather systems or the constantly recycled minerals and metals if it were not for the Moon. In other words, it might still orbit in the Goldilocks Zone but the Earth would be as dead as its companion planets were it not for the Moon.

We are the most successful species that has ever lived upon the Earth. We manipulate our environment in all manner of ways and it seems that our technological prowess knows no bounds. We have learned to build cars, spaceships, hydroelectric dams, and we have even split the atom. Our curiosity knows no bounds and we investigate the very large and the incomprehensibly small in nature with equal zeal. Is it really so far-fetched to suggest that one day we will possess the technological ability to create something like the Moon? True, it is engineering on a grand scale, but engineering nevertheless. I am an engineer and in all honesty I cannot think of any reason, other than technological advancement, that would prevent such a venture.

When we built the Moon, as I am now certain we did, we gave great thought to our long-term future. At some stage the Moon will supply us with all sorts of minerals that are getting harder to locate on Earth. Because of the natural processes that have taken place across 4 billion years, the Moon's surface is covered in helium-3. This is a wonder substance that will one day make the goal of unlimited nuclear fusion a possibility. When the oil runs out and when we finally realize that energy does not have to be dirty and polluting, helium-3 from the Moon will offer us unlimited power supplies – and all we had to do to create it was to leave the Moon spinning in space for 4 billion years!

We have spoken to several high-powered physicists about our suggestion that the Moon was man-made. They were keen enough to talk until we made the suggestion and sent them the proof. The reaction, which we have come to expect, has been silence. To paraphrase what Robert Graves said at the end of his book *The White Goddess*: 'they cannot refute it but they dare not accept it.'

So there we have it, the first and the most important intervention of them all. It will one day be necessary to send way back in time the machines that will harvest vast amounts of rock from the surface of the infant Earth. This will have to be placed in low Earth orbit – high enough not to drop back into the atmosphere but not so high it drifts off into space. There, over a long period, this rock will gradually come together to form a single body. It will have the dimensions carefully worked out for it, so that one day it can fulfil all the requirements in terms of physics, but at the same time pass on the necessary messages. Amongst these is the reality of solar eclipses, which have been described as the most unlikely scenario imaginable. True, a much denser and smaller Moon would have done the physical jobs necessary, but we could not have looked up for the last million years and marvelled at the spectacle of the Sun being eaten and then regurgitated in the middle of a sunny day.

There will be no more important intervention than this one because absolutely everything else depends upon it. All that has happened since, and all the interventions that ultimately led to the writing of this book are subservient to this one primary goal – the creation of Earth's Moon. Indeed, many of the ones I have mentioned so far, plus a couple of major ones I have yet to describe, must have been planned solely for the purpose of letting us know what we must one day achieve. The message is clear – and we may ultimately ignore it at our peril.

CHAPTER 11

New Worlds for Old

After a year-long deviation to research and write our book *Who Built the Moon?* we returned to our original research, concerned with the Megalithic system of measurement. We did so because of an unexpected lead that brought us face to face with a completely new vein of evidence, and which would serve to confirm everything we had previously suggested about Megalithic measurement.

I was made aware, thanks to a television documentary, of a structure far more recent than any Stone-Age or Bronze-Age monument, which betrayed exact Megalithic proportions. This turned out to be an 18th-century circus of houses in the southern English city of Bath. This circle of beautiful Georgian houses is known as the King's Circus, and what attracted me to it was the knowledge that its diameter was 96.6 metres. I knew immediately that this meant the circumference of the structure would be 303 metres, which I was also well aware was the same as 366 Megalithic Yards.

In *Civilization One* we had suggested that absolute proof of our theories regarding Megalithic measurement and geometry would come to light if we could find an ancient structure that was 366 Megalithic Yards, either in diameter or circumference, and suddenly we were faced with such an edifice – only this one was a mere 250 years old.

When I arrived in Bath I did some investigating – with interesting results. The King's Circus had been built by a man named John Wood, who was an architect but also a keen antiquarian. He had been particularly interested in Britain's ancient monuments. Although he had ascribed many of these to ancient mythical kings or to the Romans, Wood had done the world a great favour by carefully surveying them. This was particularly true in the case of Stonehenge, which stands on Salisbury Plain in southern England. He even produced a book itemizing his findings.

This offered an important clue. We had previously looked closely at Stonehenge ourselves. It is Britain's most famous ancient monument and consists of a number of circles and horseshoes of stones, erected across a long period of time ending around 1700BC. We had found the same Megalithic measurements in Stonehenge that Alexander Thom had discovered decades ago. Thom had stumbled across the Megalithic Yard as a component of measurements *between* stones in Megalithic monuments. This had certainly been the case at Stonehenge, which proved the existence of the Megalithic Yard in terms of the gaps between the older bluestones and the more modern sarsen stones. What Thom had not done, and neither had we, was to take note of the underlying structure at Stonehenge that is not immediately obvious. This is the 'henge' after which the site is named.

A henge is a circular structure, defined by a ditch and bank, and containing one or more entrances. Henges are to be found all over Britain. They vary greatly in size and are much earlier in date than the period when our ancestors began dragging huge stones around the landscape. Most of the henges date back to at least 3000BC.

It wasn't long before we discovered that the original henge within which the stones had been erected at Stonehenge was a perfect 366 Megalithic Yards in circumference. It was upon this part of the site that John Wood had based the dimensions for the King's Circus. We were elated. In one stroke our prophecy had been proved true – and it was concerned with what is one of the most famous ancient structures in the world.

Having been alerted to this situation we cast around Britain for other henges that we could measure. Three of the best examples lay at Thornborough in the county of Yorkshire in northern England, not far from where we both live. These henges are massive – so large indeed that London's St Paul's Cathedral could fit comfortably inside any one of them. The three henges stand in a line – huge and impressive on the landscape – and when we took measurements we found that each of them measures 732 Megalithic Yards in circumference (2 x 366 Megalithic Yards). The distance between the henges is also pertinent to our original research, being 366 Megalithic Rods between the northernmost henge and the centre henge and 360 Megalithic Rods between the centre henge and the southernmost henge.[12]

Our subsequent findings regarding the Thornborough Henge array formed the nucleus of our book *Before the Pyramids* and the findings in that book amply bear out our earlier discoveries, demonstrating absolutely that both Megalithic linear units and Megalithic geometry are hard and fast realities.

But we couldn't leave it at that. We were puzzled as to why John Wood had chosen these specific measurements. Had he simply copied the ground plan of Stonehenge, or had he somehow understood the implications of what he had done? Was he aware of the Megalithic Yard?

We knew that, in addition to being an antiquarian, John Wood (1704–54) was also an early Freemason and a member of the Ancient Order of Druids. We wondered if either of these associations had made him party to ancient knowledge that might have been somehow retained and passed on across the ages. Unfortunately John Wood died whilst he was still comparatively young, so the full extent of his prowess as an architect was never fully exploited. But was it possible, we asked ourselves, that if John Wood was an early Freemason, other members of the Craft might have also been party to the knowledge he could have possessed?

What we needed was somewhere that dated from about the same period as the King's Circus (the mid-18th century) and in which we knew Freemasons had been involved. The best example we knew about was not in Britain. Rather it was across the Atlantic in the United States of America. We were aware that Washington DC, the capital of the USA, was planned and commenced at exactly the same time the King's Circus was being built and that many of those who were responsible for its coming to reality were Freemasons.

It was one Monday morning when Chris Knight rang me and with a laugh in his voice told me he had discovered a henge in Washington DC. I knew this was an impossibility because henges don't exist outside of Britain. Nevertheless I turned to Google Earth and to the co-ordinates he gave me. Sure enough, there in front of my eyes was a structure that looked uncannily like a henge. In fact it was even more recent than the King's Circus in Bath. It was the United States Naval Observatory, which was completed in the 1880s. It had been built within a large, circular enclosure and when we measured this we were astonished to discover that the circle was 366 Megalithic Yards in diameter.

We were forced to smile. We had conjectured that the giant henges at Thornborough, and perhaps all henges, had originally been naked-eye observatories where our ancient ancestors had made themselves conversant with the night sky. Because they didn't have stones, as the later circles would, henges were in effect a blank canvas. Using wooden posts it would have been possible to create foresights and backsights of the the sort that the Megalithic people would have needed to carry out their pendulum experiments. Now, here in Washington DC, was a comparatively modern observatory, but one that conformed to the same linear measurements.

Once again we told ourselves that as interesting as this was, it might be another coincidence, so we turned our attention to the centre of Washington DC, which contains the oldest planning and structures.

For the next few days both our offices were a hive of activity. Telephone and Skype messages passed back and forth on an almost momentary basis, as we gradually came to understand what we had found.

The upshot was this – it was obvious that the whole plan for the city of Washington DC had been laid out using the Megalithic Yard as the base unit of measurement. Further to this, distances between structures (in particular road intersections, as well as the White House, the Capitol and other later creations) were definable in units of 366 Megalithic Yards, which is also the Megalithic second of arc of the Earth's polar circumference.

There were so many examples that it was impossible that this was a series of random chance events. Much earlier, when we had been researching our book *Civilization One*, we had come across the extraordinary genius Thomas Jefferson, who was the third President of the United States and the writer of the American Declaration of Independence.

Jefferson was also a scientist and toward the end of the 18th century, in 1788, he had approached the United States government (he was Secretary of State at the time) with a plan to revolutionize every aspect of the measuring systems used in the United States during the period. At this time the infant United States was fiercely independent and anxious to break its ties with Great Britain – which included the imperial measuring system. Jefferson offered nothing more or less than a completely new system, based on the length of a pendulum rod that moved back or forth in one second of time.

Long before we had considered any link with Washington DC, right back near the start of our investigations, we had realized that there was something quite strange about Jefferson's suggestions. However, we were aware that even if Thomas Jefferson had been fully conversant with the Megalithic Yard and the ½ Megalithic Yard pendulum used to define it, he could not have used this in his suggested system. This is because the Megalithic Yard is based on 366° geometry. During Jefferson's lifetime the civilized world was in love with ancient Greece. It was generally accepted that it was the ancient Greeks who had first created 360° geometry and it was already universally used by scientists and mathematicians. It could not realistically be altered or the rest of the world would think the leaders of the United States were quite mad.

Despite this, Jefferson managed to create, or at least proposed, a fully integrated measuring system within which the Megalithic Yard still existed. For example, 1,000 of the new feet Jefferson proposed is exactly equal to 360 Megalithic Yards. What is more, 366 of the much larger units he proposed, known as Jefferson Furlongs, are exactly equal to 1 Megalithic degree of the polar circumference of the Earth.

These strange facts we could not originally explain. We thought that Jefferson must have somehow 'tripped over' the Megalithic system, because of the methodology he used to create his own. We now know that this cannot have been the case. Rather, Thomas Jefferson, or somebody else, found a way to maintain the Megalithic Yard and to hide it inside another system, which was closer to the original Sumerian system of measurements.

Perhaps it wasn't too surprising then that we found so many examples of the Megalithic Yard and the Megalithic second of arc in the planning of Washington DC. There is no direct evidence that Thomas Jefferson was involved in the original planning of the city, a project that had been vouchsafed to George Washington, hero of the American War of Independence and the United States' first president. Indeed the city was eventually named after him. However, Washington and Jefferson were good friends and close colleagues – together with the fact that Jefferson had been trained as a surveyor by his father.

What did come as something of a surprise was the knowledge of where nearly all the Megalithic measurements in Washington DC originated. Just south of the White House, between it and the Mall, is an elliptical park which until very recently was known as Ellipse Park. It is now part of the President's Park. Surprise, surprise – Ellipse Park measures 366 Megalithic Yards at its widest, which is from west to east.

It is from the very centre of this Ellipse Park that most of the measurements underpinning Washington DC originate. These run from the Ellipse centre to many, if not most, of the large and impressive road intersections that were planned when the city was first envisaged. Our first discovery seemed significant because we were able to ascertain that the measurement from the centre of the Ellipse to a position right under the centre of the dome of the Capitol was 8 x 366 Megalithic Yards. The measurement was extremely accurate. This of course also represented 8 Megalithic seconds of arc of the Earth's polar circumference.

Working again from the centre of the Ellipse we carefully measured the distance to the centre of the intersections known respectively as McPherson Square and Farragut Square. These two points can be seen on the map on page 171. The distance to each was 3 x 366 Megalithic Yards. Again the results were accurate.

Further northeast of the Ellipse is Logan Circle Park. This is matched in the northwest by Dupont Circle. Both measured 6 x 366 Megalithic Yards from the Ellipse centre.

Lower to the northwest is Washington Circle Park, which prove to be 5 x 366 Megalithic Yards from the Ellipse centre. This was matched in the northeast by Mt Vernon Square, which was also 5 x 366 Megalithic Yards from the Ellipse centre.

On and on we went, until we had a dozen or more connections to the Ellipse centre, all of which resolved to a set number of units of 366 Megalithic Yards. Eventually we plotted them all on a map and the first realization was that at least some of these lines had obviously been arranged to form a very distinct and beautiful shape. It can be seen on the map on page 171 and is an elaborate arrow, pointing directly to the very centre of the Ellipse, where just under the turf is what is known as the Meridian Marker, a small cube of stone, carefully marked and placed in this position at the end of the 19th century.

Someone had gone to very great trouble to create this web of measurements that underpin the actual road network of Washington DC, and it had been done at the very start, when the first ground plan for the new city had been decided. This was slightly odd, because when the first part of Washington DC was completed, what is now the Ellipse was not an ellipse at all, but rather a piece of spare ground, surrounded by a high picket fence and known as the White Lot.

All the same, the land that would eventually become the Ellipse Park was never built on and was kept safe from development for many decades. Ellipse Park was only finally constructed shortly after the American Civil War. The work was undertaken by the Corps of Engineers, under the command of

Lieutenant Colonel Thomas Lincoln Casey. However, it is likely that Casey was working to a plan that had existed ever since the city was designed in 1791 by the Frenchman Pierre Charles L'Enfant.

The arrow formed by all the Megalithic measurements points at the dead centre of Ellipse Park and it is interesting to note that in Casey's report on the work for 1878 he noted that the land had been graded and the Ellipse set out, but that he had not done any work at the centre of the Ellipse because this land had been dug up by the 'city authorities' and did not fall under his supervision.

Why would this particular spot be so important? In fact, it is very significant indeed. When permission was first given by Congress to build Washington DC, it was stipulated that the district within which it would stand should be no more than '10 miles square'. By this the bill meant that the district should be a square, and that each side of the square could not measure more than 10 miles in length.

On a map this looks like a sort of diamond, with the corners facing north, south, east and west. The boundary was marked with carefully placed stones. If a line is drawn to connect the north corner to the south corner and another to connect the east corner to the west corner, the two lines converge over Ellipse Park. In fact the true point of crossing is just slightly to the west of the Ellipse but it is quite clear that the *intended* point of crossing was right in the middle of Ellipse Park. This is obvious because a new meridian was planned for Washington DC. This would be a line of longitude from which all other measurements in the US would be judged. This line ran right through the White House and across the middle of the Ellipse. The fact that it does not absolutely coincide with the corners of the district of Columbia is probably due to the fact that all original measurements took into account the placement of the Capitol. That had to be on a hill and this slightly altered all other measurements – bearing in mind that they were intended to be Megalithic and therefore 'fixed' in length.

In any case, surveying at the time was not the exact science it is today. At the end of the 18th century, to get the boundaries of the district as accurate as they are across rough terrain was quite an achievement.

So, at the time the Ellipse was finally turned into a park, with its present dimensions, the army could not do anything at its centre because 'someone' had dug a large hole there. What was more, the position of that hole was marked by a huge but secret arrow that had been present since Washington DC was first planned. In our book *Before the Pyramids* we speculated as to what, if anything, this hole might contain. I will come back to this in due course.

Megalithic measurements were certainly not forgotten in Washington DC once the plans had been first laid. Even by 1940 they were still being used. At the end of the 1930s the United States of America was on the verge of being drawn into a conflict that the world as a whole would not be able to avoid. President Franklin D Roosevelt, who steered the United States out of a deep depression in the 1930s, had promised the country that it would not participate in any foreign wars, but this turned out to be impossible. Not only was Nazi Germany proving to be troublesome in Europe, but the Empire of Japan was threatening to spread out from its home islands into China and Southeast Asia.

With the sky darkening it was decided that the US military would need a new base in Washington DC. Its various branches were located all round the city, which didn't make any of them particularly efficient when it came to co-operation, so a brand new headquarters building was designed. It was due to stand close to Arlington National Cemetery, across the Potomac from the centre of Washington DC and would be commenced in late 1941. At the very last minute President Roosevelt declared that the new building, to be known as the Pentagon, would not be built at Arlington Farms, but rather further south on the site of the old Hoover Airport. His generals were incensed at the sudden change in plans, but the President was also supreme commander of the armed forces and so his wishes had to be accommodated.

Of course, we measured the Pentagon, if only for the sake of thoroughness.

What we found stunned us. Not only is the Pentagon itself a perfect example of a building constructed using Megalithic measurements, its position on the landscape shows that its very centre is exactly 10 x 366 Megalithic Yards from the centre of the Ellipse and precisely 15 x 366 Megalithic Yards from the position under the dome of the Capitol. These three measurements, from the Ellipse to the Pentagon, from the Pentagon to the Capitol, and from the Capitol to the Ellipse, form a triangle that is 33 x 366 Megalithic Yards in its total length.

There is definitely a Freemasonic connection here, as we explained in *Before the Pyramids*. A pentagon is the symbol for the 32nd degree of Scottish Rite Freemasonry. Creating the Pentagon also created the giant triangle, and a triangle is the symbol for the 33rd degree of Scottish Rite Freemasonry, which is the most common form of Freemasonry in the United States. President Franklin D Roosevelt himself was a 33-degree Freemason and of course it was he who insisted on the final positioning (at the last minute) of the Pentagon, which would provide the all-important measurements and lead to the 33 Megalithic second triangle – with each Megalithic second representing 1 degree of Freemasonry. The 33rd degree is the highest degree of Scottish Rite Freemasonry and very few people ever achieve it.

There could hardly be better evidence that, in some way, an understanding of Megalithic geometry and measurement was present in Washington DC at its start, and again nearly a century and a half later, or that this retained knowledge is somehow related to Freemasonry.

Proving that the knowledge is still present in Washington DC, as recently as 2004 a new structure was opened on the Mall in Washington DC. This is the National WWII Memorial. It commemorates all Americans who fought in WWII and the 400,000 who gave their lives. It, too, has accurate Megalithic links with both the Pentagon and the Capitol, forming yet another triangle, this time a 32 Megalithic second triangle on the landscape. This is particularly appropriate because the 32nd degree of Freemasonry tells the story of a soldier, who despite having the option to stay at home and therefore remain safe, selflessly and willingly laid down his life in the service of his country and his friends.

The question remains. How is it possible that a system of measurements that disappeared from history as long ago as 1700BC, suddenly turned up again at the end of the 18th century, when there is not an inkling of it during the interim period? Did the people concerned, Freemasons of not, fully understand what they were doing, or were they simply following orders from somewhere else, or even being manipulated?

These have to be classic cases of intervention, but even these extraordinary examples are not the most striking that have occurred recently.

CHAPTER 12

A Day in September

O n Tuesday 11 September 2001 the United States experienced the most destructive series of terrorist attacks ever perpetrated in the modern world. There is absolutely no doubt that the 9/11 attacks on Washington DC and New York are and will remain one of the defining incidents of the 21st century.

Four aircraft in total were hijacked by a sizeable group of Islamic extremists and were used as 'missiles' in a series of attacks in New York and Washington that ultimately caused the deaths of nearly 3,000 people. In New York both towers of the World Trade Centre in Lower Manhattan were destroyed, whilst further south, in Washington DC, an aircraft was also flown into one of the sides of the Pentagon. A fourth aircraft, which was also destined for Washington DC (most likely the Capitol) crashed into a field near Shanksville in Pennsylvania.

Almost from the moment these attacks took place it was speculated, particularly on the internet, that the United States government had been complicit in the incidents – or was directly responsible for them. The reasons suggested are legion, but mainly centre on the fact that the administration of President George Bush was unpopular and that its credibility would be boosted if the United States had a 'cause' to follow. Conspiracy theorists suggest that the subsequent attack on Iraq that took place under the guise of eliminating Al Qaeda and also supposed weapons of mass destruction was actually a diversionary measure, intended to divert attention from an inept Presidency, short on ideas but big on jingoism. Many conspiracy theorists also see the whole scenario as part of a 'one-world government' strategy in which the United States administration is a willing participant.

My own personal opinion, and I suspect that of most rational people, is that the 9/11 attacks were exactly what they appeared to be – the work of a small group of fundamentalist fanatics, who thought up a plan that turned out to be more successful than even they could have hoped. To suggest that the whole thing was an American government conspiracy seems ultimately absurd, if only because the vast number of people involved in such a plan would have been so great it would have proved impossible to keep everyone silent afterwards. In this age of 'whistle-blowing' I find it to be extremely telling that not one person who had the slightest involvement at any level in the supposed conspiracy has come forward to report the fact. It sometimes seems, in the case of 9/11, that the need for such a conspiracy stems in part from a sense of incredulity that these events could ever have been allowed to take place. If the government of the United States was guilty of anything, it was not an involvement in the horrors but rather a complete failure in its ability to monitor what Al Qaeda was so carefully planning for so long.

The investigations by Christopher Knight and myself into Washington DC took place some years after the 9/11 attacks. The telling measurements we had discovered all across the city dealt with decisions that had been taken toward the end of the 18th century and again immediately before the outbreak of the Second World War. What connection could there possibly be between our own investigations and the horrors of that Tuesday in 2001? The answer is a very strange one, and I believe it lies at the very heart of the theory of intervention.

Running roughly northeast from the very centre of Washington DC is the road known for many decades as New York Avenue. It commences at an inter-section with Pennsylvania Avenue, not far from the northern entrance to the White House. If a direct line is taken from the centre of Ellipse Park to Lower

Manhattan, New York, the distance is close to 204 miles (329 kilometres). This might seem entirely arbitrary but, in fact, it is far from being so. I checked this distance because I wanted to know whether other major centres in the United States had been as deliberately placed as had Washington DC, but I could hardly have expected to come to the result I did. From the centre of Washington's Ellipse Park to the centre of the South Tower of the World Trade Centre the distance is 203.77 miles (327.94 kilometres). When turned into Megalithic measurements something becomes immediately obvious. This distance represents exactly 3 Megalithic degrees of the Earth's polar circumference.

All the relevant measurements we had found in Washington DC were multiples of 366 Megalithic Yards, which is itself 1 Megalithic second of arc of the Earth's polar circumference. The distance between Ellipse Park centre and the South Tower of the World Trade Centre equals 1,080 such units. There are 6 Megalithic seconds of arc to 1 Megalithic minute of arc and 60 Megalithic minutes of arc to 1 Megalithic degree of arc, so 1,080 Megalithic seconds of arc equals 3 Megalithic degrees.

Could this be a coincidence? Of course it could. Almost anything *could be* a coincidence. A more relevant question might be – is this *likely* to be a coincidence? The reader could be forgiven for declaring that a coincidence is the only possible answer for this result. After all, what possible connection could there be between a park that was envisaged in Washington DC at the end of the 18th century and made a reality in the 19th century, and a structure that was opened in New York in 1973? But when all the facts are taken into account I would suggest that a coincidence is not the most likely explanation at all.

Conspiracy theorists who speculate as to the *real* motivation for the 9/11 attacks and come to the conclusion that it was part of a US government conspiracy may be wide of the mark, but there are facts concerning the attacks that do deserve more attention; in particular the attack on the Pentagon in Washington DC and the intended attack on either the Capitol or the White

House that resulted in a spectacular plane crash in Pennsylvania.

Despite the damage to the Pentagon when American Airlines Flight 77 slammed into the building, it is almost certain that the US authorities breathed a sigh of relief regarding this aspect of the 9/11 events. This is because the aircraft hit the west side of the Pentagon, and not any of the other four sides. In 1998 an extensive programme of rebuilding and upgrading began at the Pentagon. This was necessary because when the building was completed in the 1940s, it had been decided that the construction should be mostly of concrete – in order to save on the use of steel, which was needed for the war effort. As a result, the finished building, though vast in size, was not especially strong. At the time of the Second World War this was not an issue. Neither Nazi Germany nor Japan had bombers or missiles capable of travelling the vast distance to the United States, so aerial attack was not a consideration at the time of the Pentagon's planning.

Through the long years of the Cold War it was probably considered unnec-essary to upgrade the Pentagon. After all, if nuclear war had taken place, no amount of strengthening would have protected the building from such a potential attack. Indeed, the very centre of the Pentagon had a café that was laughingly named 'Ground Zero Café' because it was gruesomely considered this would be the point upon which the first Russian missile would fall. A nuclear explosion in this location would not only have totally destroyed the Pentagon, but probably Washington DC as a whole.

Times change and the Oklahoma bombings that took place in the United States in 1995 acted as a wake-up call to the US administration that terrorist attacks could take place on United States soil, and the Pentagon seemed to be a first-line target. So it was decided that the whole building should be massively upgraded. This was commenced in 1998 and the first 'wedge' of the building upgraded was the one that faced west. Significant steel strength-ening was added, together with virtually indestructible Kevlar support and extremely thick toughened glass in the windows. A new and efficient sprinkler system was installed and many new safety features added. At the time of the

9/11 attack, this wedge of the Pentagon was nearing completion – but it was not yet finished, and so although there were an estimated 20,000 people in the building, only a few hundred were in this section.

The outer wall of the wedge held up extremely well to the impact of the aircraft and did not collapse for nearly 30 minutes after the attack – thus affording the few people who were there time to escape. The aircraft penetrated the E Ring (outer ring) of the wedge and pushed on into the D Ring and the C Ring beyond. The damage was extensive but nowhere near as bad as would undoubtedly have been the case if the impact had taken place on any of the other four as yet unstrengthened wedges. In total 125 occupants of the Pentagon died, together with the 58 passengers and crew of the aircraft, but as tragic as this was it was a drop in the ocean compared with the likely death toll if the terrorists had chosen to target a different wedge.

The alterations made to the western wedge of the Pentagon had been extensive. It is almost certain if the impact had taken place anywhere else on the building, none of which had yet been strengthened at all, the aircraft would have continued through all five rings of the building and into the central area beyond. If there were 20,000 people in the building, there must have been an average of 5,000 in each of the unmodified wedges! As a result, more people could quite easily have died in the Pentagon than perished at the Twin Towers of the World Trade Centre.

The two important questions here are: why did the terrorists in command of Flight 77 choose the western wedge of the Pentagon to hit; and why should there be any Megalithic connection between the location of the centre of Washington DC and the Twin Towers of the World Trade Centre in New York? Could it be that both of these facts owe as much to our future as they do to our past?

I now want to look at the situation from the point of view of those looking back at it from the near or distant future. The laws governing intervention demonstrate that even when time travel becomes a possibility from a practical point of view, it will be impossible to alter any event that has taken place in the past. As I have pointed out, it is only possible to visit periods in the past where one was actually present. However, this does not mean there can be no 'involvement' in past events because in some cases that involvement actually did take place and so becomes a part of the historic timeline.

I believe that this could quite easily be the case with regard to the incidents that took place on 11 September 2001. As I look back on those events now, I can see, as can everyone else, just how easily the whole business could have been subverted. Better surveillance of potentially dangerous foreign nationals; more intense observation of Al Qaeda; better airport security on United States internal flights and better co-ordination of military air cover above Washington DC and New York could all have contributed to making certain no such tragedy could ever take place. However, it is too late for any of these eventualities; 9/11 happened and it cannot be 'un-happened' no matter how much we or our future selves would wish it so.

All the same, when one bears in mind the events as they actually played out on the day, it is possible to see that intervention may well have taken place and that this intervention could actually have halved the number of fatalities. For future interventionists looking back on these events, there would be no point in lamenting the failures, but they might analyse what actually happened and see ways in which intervention 'could' take place and therefore most likely 'did' take place, to lessen the impact of the attacks. It would then be necessary to travel back in time and to implement certain actions that do synchronize with the historical reality of that day.

Chief amongst these would be the strengthening of the western wedge of the Pentagon, which was planned and commenced three years before 9/11. The chance of those flying the aircraft that plunged into the Pentagon choosing this particular wedge was 1 in 5. Why this wedge was chosen by the terrorists is not known. The land around the Pentagon is fairly flat, though it does rise to the north and the buildings of Washington DC itself might have made this particular approach difficult. However, approaches from the south or the east would not have been especially problematic. Perhaps the approach from the west was chosen because immediately to the west of the Pentagon is Arlington National Cemetery and a good deal of open land without the number of buildings that would be encountered when flying low toward the Pentagon from other directions.

Was it simply good luck that the wedge into which the terrorists decided to fly was the only one that had been strengthened, and also the only one where very few people were present on the day in question? Was it, as some people suggest, the will of God? If so, why was the loss of life at the World Trade Centre so great? Or was something else at work? Will our future selves look at the situation carefully and realize, as I have done, that there was indeed a series of interventions that would be quite possible, without interfering with history at all, that taken together would significantly lessen the blow of 9/11?

If this was indeed the case, those undertaking the necessary interventions must have been involved at some level in the planning that took place regarding the strengthening of the Pentagon, three years before 9/11. Either by having representatives present in the various bodies and committees that instigated the Pentagon's strengthening, or by manipulating those who were part of the committees, they would have had to make sure that:

1 The strengthening of the Pentagon was sanctioned and that it began in 1998.
2 That the first wedge of the Pentagon to be strengthened would be the one facing west.

In both cases, interventionists from the future could have been totally responsible for the decisions that were taken regarding the Pentagon and, of course, they could take these decisions with the benefit of hindsight. They already knew that the aircraft would hit the west-facing wedge of the Pentagon and they were also aware that this was the only section of the building that had been substantially altered and strengthened. It merely remained for them to intervene in such a way that history was played out as it ultimately was. These were actions they could take because by doing so they were not seeking to *alter* history, but merely to confirm it.

They may also have been responsible for what happened to United Airlines Flight 93 because, as American Airlines Flight 77 banked steeply to make its approach on the western side of the Pentagon, another hijacked aircraft was also heading for Washington DC. United Airlines Flight 93 had taken off on an intended journey from Newark, New Jersey to San Francisco International Airport. Around 46 minutes after the aircraft had left New Jersey, it was hijacked – but the scenario in this case was slightly different from the two aircraft that hit the World Trade Centre. Passengers aboard the plane had cell phones and they received information from colleagues and relatives concerning the attacks on the World Trade Centre in New York. It did not take them long to work out that the fate of their own aircraft was likely to be the same as those that had hit the Twin Towers. As a result, a number of the passengers determined to overpower the hijackers and, if possible, take back the plane. These brave people no doubt realized that they were doomed in any case, so that at the very least if they could overpower the terrorists they could avoid more casualties on the ground. Ultimately, the aircraft crashed in Shanksville Pennsylvania. All the passengers and crew, together with the hijackers were killed, but if the plane had continued to its intended target, which is certain to have been in Washington and was probably the Capitol, many more innocent people would have died.

However, despite their monumental courage, there is great doubt about whether it was the passengers who caused Flight 93 to crash. Conspiracy theorists claim it was shot down by United States military aircraft, but there is no real evidence to support this supposition. The flight recorders were salvaged from the wreckage and these have left a testimony of the conversations that took place in the cockpit between the hijackers. They seemed to be aware that the passengers were attempting to storm the front of the aircraft, but there is no evidence from the flight recorders that they succeeded. Ultimately, for whatever reason, United Airlines Flight 93 crashed at over 500mph at 10.03am.

Once again we need to look at this situation from the perspective of those viewing it as a historical event. The facts are that the aircraft was hijacked and that it crashed in Pennsylvania. Simply because it crashed and because it did not reach its intended target, it has to be a possibility that the demise of the Boeing 757, like the strengthening of the Pentagon, came as the result of an intervention from the future. Those arranging this eventuality could hardly be considered to be murderers. The aircraft did crash, and its passengers and crew were doomed to die on that morning. But because it came down in a very rural location, many hundreds of other lives in Washington DC were undoubtedly saved. To have arranged such an eventuality would surely not have been difficult for people who had mastered time travel, and it could have been achieved in a number of different ways.

What I see as most interesting in terms of possible interventions associated with 9/11 is the fact that our future selves were able to inform us of their presence and influence on that horrific day, and what is more, they did so in such a way that the only possible explanation was that people who could travel in time had been responsible. The astounding Megalithic connection between that all-important spot at the centre of the Washington DC Ellipse Park, and the centre of the South Tower of the World Trade Centre was engineered as early as 1961 when the billionaire David Rockefeller suggested that a World Trade Centre (that had been proposed for New York as early as 1943) should be placed in Lower Manhattan.

The Rockefeller family have been of interest to Christopher Knight and me for some time, and I propose to say more about them in the following chapter.

Placing the World Trade Centre where it stood ensured that it immediately locked into the same sort of relationship with the centre of the Ellipse in Washington DC enjoyed by iconic structures in Washington itself, including the White House, the Capitol and of course the Pentagon. It makes the whole association between these locations, and the events that took place on 9/11, yet another 'message in a bottle'. It says, in the words of our future selves – 'We were here and we had something to do with all of this.'

Of course there is a paradoxical sting in the tail to this particular part of my story; 9/11 did happen, and it happened exactly in the way our newsreels and newspapers reported at the time. No detail of what took place can ever be altered. We may not understand every minor twist, turn or nuance of the story but to all intents and purposes it is irrevocably locked into the timeline of humanity and of our world. In this sense it might be suggested that even if our future selves did play a part in potentially saving possibly thousands of lives on that fateful day, in reality they had no choice. Their ultimate actions were as inevitable as those of the misguided and, in my opinion, sick individuals who took command of the four aircraft.

Does this somehow make us all the pawns of fate? I may be wrong but I don't think this is the case. It is all dependent on the way we view time and the way it works. What we don't know, and can never know, is what would have happened during those horrible hours if our future selves had not been involved at all. Might we now be looking back on a catastrophe of much greater proportions? I cannot claim to know the answer to this question. Stuck in our own particular part of the timeline, we can only view the history we have. We might interpret and reinterpret its significance to ourselves, but for the sake of our own sanity we should perhaps accept that it remains inevitable and immutable.

CHAPTER 13

The Future as a Reflection of the Past

I f intervention from the future into the past, both recent and remote, really has taken place, we should expect to see 'clues'. It might appear that even huge periods of time have been 'bracketed' by common events – even though there is no tangible, logical connection between them. The existence of the Megalithic measuring system prior to 2000BC, and then its mysterious appearance in late 18th-century Washington DC, could be a case in question. But it is far from being the only example. History is littered with oddities that only really make sense in light of intervention theory.

By what might seem to be merely a twist of fate, nearly 30 years ago I began what has become a life-long relationship with a specific region of France. The Yorkshire town to which I moved in the 1970s happened to be twinned with another town, in northern France. The name of the French twin was Montereau-Fault-Yonne, not far south of Paris and close to the northern part of the region known as Champagne.

I became part of the twinning committee and so began a regular series of journeys to Montereau-Fault-Yonne, where I came to know many of the people there and ultimately became close friends with a few. Twinning trips gave way to holidays and, since my hosts knew of my fondness for history, they began to take us to places in the region that they thought would be of interest to me. This is how I was first introduced to Troyes, once the capital city of Champagne and a place that I now recognize had a unique part to play in the development of Western Europe and, ultimately, the world as a whole.

Toward the end of the 11th century Christianity was in turmoil. After the effective break-up of the Roman Empire, Christianity, which had been adopted by Rome around AD325, disappeared from some regions but proliferated in other areas, with its two major centres located in Rome itself and in Constantinople. As time passed, Christianity began to spread again, into the far-flung regions of Western Europe, such as France and the British Isles, but a singular threat was developing in the Middle East.

In the 6th century AD a new religion sprang up, in and around the Persian Gulf. It had grown from the same root as Judaism and Christianity, but it would become an implacable enemy to both. This belief pattern was and is known as Islam. It was begun by a prophet whose name was Mohammed and during his life (AD570–630) but especially after, Islam began to spread rapidly, first across the Middle East but then out into the soft underbelly of Europe.

The invasion of Spain by Islamic forces began in 711 and within a decade the whole of the Spanish peninsula had been conquered. This was of immense concern to the leaders of Christianity, especially in Rome. For a while it looked as though France would also fall to Islam as Septimania, the old name for Visigoth southern France, was also briefly conquered by Islamic forces. Christianity began to fight back and Charles Martel, King of the Franks, pushed the Muslims back over the mountains into Spain. His successor, Charlemagne, began to wrest Spain from Islamic domination and Western Europe was free from the threat, but further East things were quite different.

Islam pushed into Eastern Europe and eventually began to threaten the other major area of Christian influence – Byzantium. Historically speaking, the Christian rulers in Constantinople had not got on particularly well with their Roman counterparts but, nevertheless, toward the end of the 11th century, they made a plea to the pope in Rome to come to their assistance with all necessary speed, because Constantinople itself was in danger.

The pope at the time, Urban II, was happy to oblige, partly because he had problems of his own. The feudal nature of much of Western Christendom was proving to be a thorn in the side of Roman Christianity. Western Europe was filled with armed warriors, all of whom were avaricious for land and power and who made life intolerable for ordinary people and for the Church with their constant fighting. It must have occurred to Pope Urban II that if he could pack off all these heavily armed sons of petty and great lords on some foreign adventure, they would have a cause for their sword arms and Christianity might benefit as a result. In 1095 the pope gave a speech at Claremont in France, in which he called on all Christians to take part in a holy war against Islam, which he hoped would take the pressure off Byzantium and also capture, for Christianity, the holy places of the Middle East, and in particular Jerusalem.

What followed was the First Crusade, and in 1099 the forces of Western Christianity, led by Godfroi de Bouillon, stormed over the walls of Jerusalem and took the city from the Muslims. Such was their success that they ultimately conquered much of the Near East, but it was not a state of affairs that lasted very long because within two centuries the Islamic forces had regrouped and the whole region was once again lost to Christianity.

No region of Western Europe benefited more from the Crusades than Champagne. Nominally speaking it was a vassal state of the kings of France, but in reality it was autonomous and was ruled by a dynasty of counts. Champagne stood at a series of important crossroads and marked a meeting point for merchants from the north and those from Italy and beyond. With the opening up of the Middle East, luxury goods from formerly exotic places began to pour into Western Europe and the markets of Champagne were the chief beneficiaries of all this trade.

Seen with the benefit of hindsight, it becomes obvious that what took place in Champagne after the beginning of the 12th century did not simply represent a region accidentally benefiting from a set of circumstances beyond its own control, but rather a series of deliberate decisions, instigated within

Champagne for its own benefit, but ultimately having a significant bearing on the whole known world of the time.

Firstly, the nobility of Champagne was active in the proposal for a Crusade that could bring the Middle East into the Christian fold to take place. Both its count and a large number of his vassals took part in the First Crusade. Godfroi de Bouillon, who led the Crusaders into Jerusalem and who effectively became the first Christian king of the city, was blood-tied to the counts of Champagne; and the Count of Champagne himself, with his immediate followers, was at Godfroi's side as they stormed into Christianity's most holy location.

Just as soon as Jerusalem was secure, a series of moves were made in Champagne that would see the little region benefiting mightily from the situation and the ultimate result was a complete change in the way Western Europe began to develop. At each stage on this remarkable journey one gets the impression that those ordering events in and around Champagne were working to a definite and quite cohesive plan – pushing an agenda that appeared to support the religious and political status quo, when in reality they were doing something far different. One has to wonder if their actions were in some way being influenced by outside agencies and question whether intervention theory might explain the extraordinary series of events that took place. People from the future could make great sense out of what, in any specific 'present', might be confusing or impossible to interpret.

The four major moves taken in the months and years immediately before and following the First Crusade, which ultimately led to the world we live in today were:

1. Prior to the call for the First Crusade, Champagne was able to gain control of the papacy in Rome. The Champagne aristocrat who was made pope in 1088 was Odo of Lagery, a blood relative of the counts of Champagne from Châtillon-sur-Marne. It was this man, as Urban II, whose actions led to the First Crusade.

2. The creation of a series of year-round markets in Champagne that would attract merchants from far and wide. These were known as the Champagne fairs.

3. The creation of a new monastic order that worked in a way far different to anything that had gone before. The members of this order were known as the Cistercians.

4. The creation of an armed extension to the Cistercian order, which would be known to history as the Knights Templar and which would quickly become something far more important than a bunch of fanatical holy soldiers.

Control of the papacy was clearly the first necessary strategy in a series of carefully laid plans because Christendom had to be prepared to join forces in order to secure Jerusalem and the Middle East. Only a pope had the power to call to arms many thousands of men from different countries, and to send them off on such an adventure. This is precisely what Urban II did in 1095.

Whilst Odo of Lagery was doing what was expected of him in Rome, the counts of Champagne spent vast sums of money on the Champagne fairs. They organized the venues in the different towns of Champagne, with great warehouses and accommodation for those taking part. In addition they arranged for the economic requirements of the merchants, effectively creating banks and credit facilities, as well as ensuring that the events were skilfully and efficiently policed so that those participating could feel safe. The Fairs attracted timber and fur merchants from Scandinavia and the Baltic, wool merchants from Flanders and Britain, merchants bringing luxury goods from Italy, and those responsible for even more sumptuous and exotic merchandise from the Middle East and the Silk Road beyond. All of these participants could come together on a regular basis to exchange goods and to create mercantile possibilities that could not have been dreamed of previously.

The Cistercian order of monks was created by another noble relative of the counts of Champagne. His name was Robert of Molesme. He was born around 1028 or 1029 and began his monastic career at Montier-la-Celle, near Troyes. Robert was dissatisfied with the monastic status quo of his time; he thought the Benedictine order had become lax and decadent. As a result he sought to found a new order. This came about in 1098 – as the armies of the Crusade were about to lay siege to far-off Jerusalem. The Cistercian order that he formed probably affected the modern world more than any other institution before or since.

The first Cistercians were left to struggle along at their founding abbey in northern Burgundy until another blood-relative of the counts of Champagne was ready for his assigned task. This was Bernard of Clairvaux, whose father Tescelin had been at the right hand of Godfroi de Bouillon during the storming of Jerusalem. As soon as he was old enough, Bernard joined the infant Cistercian order, together with over 30 of his relatives. Within a couple of years he was effectively in control of the order – so much so that an alternative name for the Cistercians was the 'Bernardines'. Bernard, later St Bernard of Clairvaux, effectively ran the Cistercian order from his own abbey at Clairvaux, close to Troyes. He was a skilled statesman, a peerless innovator, a shrewd businessman, and probably the most influential individual of his period. Bernard of Clairvaux was also a pope-maker and had the ear of kings and emperors across most of Western Europe.

Yet another kinsman of the counts of Champagne was responsible for the formation of the Knights Templar. His name was Hugh de Payens and his lands lay within the boundaries of the city of Troyes. Hugh had fought with distinction in the First Crusade and, if history is to be believed, together with a group of associates he presented himself at the palace of the new Christian kings of Jerusalem around 1119. He announced that he and his companions wanted to form a militia that could protect pilgrims on the road between the Mediterranean coast and Jerusalem; the then king, Baldwin II, granted the small band land immediately adjacent to his own palace on the Temple Mount at the heart of Jerusalem. The new order then disappears from history for a full decade.

It is worth mentioning at this point in the story that a friend of mine, Tim Beswick, is a great advocate of what he calls 'the cock-up theory of history'. As a historian himself he suggests that by far most of what happens throughout the centuries comes about as a result of circumstances that are more or less beyond our control – they are generally the result of happenstance. In many cases I have to agree with Tim, but there are notable examples, such as what took place in northern France at this pivotal time, that seem to owe nothing to accident and everything to a sort of systematic planning that could only have taken place not just *somewhere else* but also *sometime else*.

A few years elapsed whilst Bernard of Clairvaux gradually gained power within the Church and, in particular, influence with the pope. Then, in 1129 a great Church Council was held in Troyes, Champagne, during which Pope Honorius II declared Hugh de Payens and his colleagues to be an official monastic order. He placed them under the guidance of Bernard of Clairvaux and they became known as the Poor Knights of Christ and the Temple of Solomon (the Knights Templar). This was really a case of 'calling in favours' by Bernard of Clairvaux because the fact that Honorius II was pope at all, rather than a rival candidate, Celestine II, was chiefly due to Bernard's influence.

Almost immediately the Knights Templar began to expand at lightning speed. They were indeed soldiers and fought with distinction, but they soon became much more. In a short while the Templars were shippers, traders, bankers and massive power brokers amongst the crowned heads of Europe and beyond. It was from the time of the Council of Troyes – from 1129 onward – that the ultimate plans so carefully laid in Champagne were put into action.

The Cistercian monks adopted a two-tier approach to monasticism. In each abbey there were choir monks, who officiated at the altar but who were also expected to work, and there were lay brothers, whose main role was to do the manual work, of which there was a great deal. Cistercians chose areas of waste land that nobody wanted, but they soon made such areas into rich and productive farm land. The secret of their success lay in sheep rearing, at which they were excellent. In Britain, especially, each of their monasteries ran tens of thousands of sheep. The sheep could survive on the marginal land, all the time improving it with their dung and eventually allowing it to be planted with crops. Each year the sheep were shorn and the wool was sent to Flanders, from where it was worked and then transhipped to Champagne. At the Champagne fairs it was sold into the Italian markets and ultimately found its way much further east, or else was reworked as quality fabric and came back via the Champagne fairs to the West. Wool made the Cistercians a fortune, which was ploughed back into the order, as dozens of new Cistercian houses were built. In the end the Cistercians were the most successful Christian monastic order that ever existed. In addition to being excellent farmers they were also engineers, builders, woodworkers, smiths and great miners of coal, iron and other metals; they drained huge quantities of land in Flanders and East Anglia in England, and also created ports from which their wool could be transhipped.

As the Cistercians gradually built up their holdings in Europe, the Knights Templar reaped the benefits and added more to the overall strategy that had been planned in Troyes. Building a huge fleet of ships, the Templars travelled across the known world, shipping cargoes and passengers, and building and guarding roads. They became great traders but they also served another vitally important role – as bankers. The Templars effectively invented cheque-book banking, were great money lenders – often to kings and emperors – and they were the chief tax collectors for crowned heads and popes. The Templars were builders on a vast scale and were as good at farming as their cousins the Cistercians. Because they were based in Troyes, Champagne, the Templars stood at the heart of the success of the Champagne fairs. Their own wool, together with that of the Cistercians, formed the core merchandise at the fairs and they invariably supervised its transhipment, which also added to the fortune they were making. Both the Cistercians and the Templars reported directly to the popes and so were exempt from local taxes or any sort of influence from the rulers of states in which they had holdings. In effect, they became totally autonomous.

For reasons that are still not totally understood, the Knights Templar eventually fell foul of many of the rulers of Western Europe – though in reality it isn't hard to see why. They were owed vast sums of money and the kings of France in particular came to reason that if the Templars went away, so would the debts. In 1307, on what were probably mostly trumped-up charges, the Templars were arrested all over France. The pope at the time was a French puppet, so the inevitable conclusion was that the Templars were declared heretical and were disbanded. Meanwhile, the Cistercian order had become as lax and decadent as the Benedictines had been, so that by the time of the Reformations of the 16th century the order was a shadow of its former self.

None of this mattered because a very important cat had been let out of the bag and nobody would ever be able to entice it back in. What the Champagne fairs, the Cistercians and the Knights Templar had done between them was to completely change the face of international relations and trade within Europe and beyond. When the Templars were disbanded, their fantastic banking and shipping empire simply passed into other hands and the trading went on much as before. Even the demise of the importance of the Champagne fairs did nothing to slow down the mercantile revolution that was taking place. Feudal leaders were less and less able to see themselves as totally independent because they were starting to become members of a much larger, international community, and their economies were now dependent on foreign trade. Ultimately this also led to a spread of information, to better education, to fabulously rich merchants who sought to promote art and culture, and eventually to a full-blown Renaissance. In due course this also led to a form of secularism that began to break the iron-hard grip of Roman Catholicism.

The consequences of the original plan to elevate Champagne from its former state, as a rural backwater, to that of major international player, had already been monumental. However, time would show that what had taken place so far was as nothing in comparison with what would follow. Was it all as a result of a series of coincidences, or was there something far more remarkable at work?

In Britain the exertions of the Cistercians and the Templars had completely changed the landscape. At the time of the Reformation the vast Cistercian lands passed into private hands – but the populace had learned a great deal from the White Monks and continued to farm the land as the Cistercians had done. Ultimately, the Cistercian drive to *enclose* land became the norm and it led to a great agricultural revolution in Britain, which ultimately financed the Industrial Revolution that followed it. Almost all the early industrial ventures were brought about because of money earned from wool.

Readers who want to know more about this almost completely overlooked but fantastically important period of European history might want to read my books *The Goddess, the Grail and the Lodge*[13] and *Sheep*[14] in order to get a fuller explanation of all that took place.

Quite remarkably, bearing in mind the intensely feudal nature of the world at the time, all of what the Cistercians and the Templars achieved was the product of two very democratic institutions and represented Western Europe's first flirtation with democracy since the days of the ancient Greeks. Officers of both the Cistercian, and the Templar orders, were elected from within the organizations by the brothers themselves; ultimately, the lowliest choir monk or Templar Knight, had a daily say, at an institution called 'Chapter', in the way his organization was run. Democracy of this sort would not be seen again in Western Europe until four or five hundred years later.

For a while, and in no short measure thanks to the Cistercians and the Templars, Great Britain became the powerhouse of the world and came to control an empire that made the Roman Empire look feeble in comparison. Amongst the British Empire's most prized possessions were the settlements along the eastern seaboard of North America, which, when they gained independence at the end of the 18th century, formed themselves into the United States of America. The new United States took the best of the British system of government and built upon it – creating a nation that prized democracy above everything and which eventually became the most powerful country the world has ever known.

From the very start the byword of the United States was liberty, and the founding fathers were particularly keen to ensure that no religious creed should be allowed to have any part to play in the governance of what was truly a secular state. This is not to suggest that religion has not participated in the building of the United States, but men such as George Washington, Benjamin Franklin, and particularly Thomas Jefferson, fought like tigers to prevent the United States legislature from being influenced by any particular religious belief or affiliation. However, had it not been for the Champagne adventure of the 11th to the 14th century, Britain would never have risen to prominence, and control over both North and South America would undoubtedly have fallen to deeply Catholic states such as Spain, Portugal and France.

All of this represents part of what, for the last decade and more, I have been calling 'the Continuum'. If one is unfettered by the traditional way of viewing history and dismisses the notion that ultimately everything happens entirely by chance, it is possible to discern within the twists and turns of world history what I have also called 'the golden thread through the tapestry of time'.

Connections occur between groups and institutions, some of which are divorced by vast periods of time. As I suggested at the start of this chapter, the fact that Megalithic measurements were used in the planning of Washington DC, after having been missing from the historical record for nearly 4,000 years, is a good example. Looking back at history it is possible to discern groups of people with specific ideas and intentions – such as the democratic values of the Cistercians and the Templars, which were totally out of kilter with the time in which they emerged. And always when the golden thread breaks through to shine brightly against the backdrop of mundane events, we can perceive people of great power and intellect, whose ideas and ideals have a commonality that should not be expected as a matter of course.

Sometimes the power to perpetuate ideas about liberty and the natural place of religion, in a world filled with people who have differing beliefs, surfaces in strange places. Probably the best example of this is the institution of Freemasonry, the origins of which are worthy of one or more books in their own right. I refer readers to my own book *The Goddess, the Grail and the Lodge*[15] and to a book I wrote with Christopher Knight entitled *The Hiram Key Revisited.*[16]

For an institution that most people think of as being 'secret' and somewhat 'cranky and odd', Freemasonry has had a tremendous part to play in the building of the modern world. It would be quite impossible in this chapter to itemize just how important Freemasonry has been, but aside from the part it has played in the general running of the world across the last two or three centuries, it was most probably responsible for both the American and the French Revolutions, and the United States of America stands square on Masonic principles. This is a fact that is deplored by many fundamentalist Christians in the US – but it is a fact nevertheless.

Freemasonry is a legacy of organizations such as the Knights Templar. Its aims and objectives are generally philanthropic and though it is often cited as being against religious belief this is certainly not the case. No man (or woman these days) can participate in Freemasonry unless they are willing to acknowledge a belief in an all-powerful deity. The hatred of Freemasonry, particularly from the direction of the Catholic Church, stems from the fact that Freemasons are not asked to acknowledge the God of Christianity specifically.

I do not intend to provide an 'apology' for Freemasonry. I am not a Freemason myself and so have no particular axe to grind. I seek only to report 'what is' and this includes a recognition that there is something deeply significant about Freemasonry and Freemasonic practice that forms part of a continuum that has been surfacing and resurfacing in the world for possibly thousands of years. Freemasonry is not a religion but more a philosophy. Like the founding fathers of the United States (many of whom were Freemasons), it seeks to allow each of its members to become the very best individuals they can be – and on the way, Freemasonry raises countless dollars each year for charities that are both Masonic and non-Masonic. After more than a decade of looking so carefully at the institution, I can only think that Freemasonry is so hated and despised in some quarters simply because it is unfettered by religious or political constraints. Freemasons are accused of being devil worshippers. This is absurd, but it is also suggested that they have played and still play a clandestine role in directing the world. Even though the average Freemason would laugh at such a suggestion, years of careful research have taught me that this particular accusation is essentially correct.

It is also possible to recognize certain dynasties or families that seem to be associated with the Continuum. Christopher Knight and I called these people 'the Star Families' and have suggested that they can trace their lineage far, far back in time – in fact right back to the pre-Judaic patriarchs such as Enoch and Noah and before the commencement of world religions as we know them today. Such families display certain characteristics, particularly of belief. I am not the first person to recognize these individuals. The English writer Anthony Trollope (1815–82) was a great social commentator and also himself a Freemason. In one of his books he describes a character by the name of Dr Thorne (who incidentally seems to have much in common with Trollope himself). This is what Trollope wrote about Dr Thorne – it is very telling.

> He, however, [Dr Thorne] and others around him, who still maintained the same staunch principles of protection – Men like himself, who were too true to flinch at the cry of a mob – had their own way of consoling themselves. They were, and felt themselves to be, the only true depositories left of certain Eleusinian Mysteries, of certain deep and wondrous services of worship by which alone the Gods could be rightly approached. To them and them only was it now given to know these things, and to perpetuate them, if that might still be done, by the careful and secret education of their children.
>
> We have read how private and peculiar forms of worship have been carried on from age to age in families, which to the outer world have apparently adhered to the services of some ordinary

church. And so it was by degrees with Mr Thorne. He learned at
length to listen calmly while protection was talked of as a thing
dead, although he knew within himself that it was still quick
with a mystic life. Nor was he without a certain pleasure that
such knowledge, though given to him, should be debarred from
the multitude.[17]

Dr Thorne was, of course, a fictional character, but similarity of thought and
purpose can be seen in real-life individuals and families. One such family is
the Rockefellers.

The Rockefellers are one of the richest families in the world, their initial
wealth having come from Standard Oil. The present patriarch of the family,
David Rockefeller, was born in 1915 into a family that was already extremely
wealthy and influential. Conspiracy theorists are always keen to point the finger
at David Rockefeller. He is often accused of being a member of a shadowy
organization known as the 'Illuminati', which has been supposedly directing
major events in the world for centuries. Probably the greatest criticism of
David Rockefeller stems from his involvement in the creation of 'the Trilateral
Commission', a so-called think tank that exists to foster better co-operation
and understanding between the United States, Western Europe and Japan.

Those people, mainly in the United States, who are virtually paranoid about
the idea that there are powerful people across the globe whose intention is
the create and oversee a 'one-world government', suggest that the Trilateral
Commission is an organization specifically designed to work toward such
an objective.

Be that as it may, David Rockefeller is the man most responsible not only
for the World Trade Centre having existed, but for its specific location in
Lower Manhattan. He ranks as one of the most influential people in the world
today, has donated hundreds of millions of dollars to charities and institutions of his own choosing and has, during his long life, rubbed shoulders
with the good and the great across the globe. His immediate ancestors were

responsible for creating the Rockefeller Foundation. This is a philanthropic organization which, since the first part of the 20th century, has been instrumental in promoting education across the world, has striven hard to eradicate disease and squalor, has promoted better international understanding, and has worked to promote and support all manner of cultural projects, as well as providing funds for laureates and even creating universities.

As advanced as they were in forming their Foundation, the Rockefellers were not the first to suggest such a plan. That accolade belongs to Benjamin Franklin, one of the original founding fathers of the United States and a man who was present when Washington DC was planned and first built. He was a friend of both George Washington and Thomas Jefferson and had similar political and religious beliefs.

Charitable as it may be, the Rockefeller Foundation falls foul of some groups, again especially in the United States. In the past it has promoted a better understanding of *all* world religions, which has agitated at least some Christian fundamentalists, and it has also championed efforts in contraception, geared toward reducing the size of the Earth's human population. This certainly does not please all Christians and neither does the fact that it has been responsible for bodies that have accepted the need for abortion under certain circumstances.

In general it seems that the attitude taken by the Rockefeller Foundation toward religion has been very similar to that adopted by the majority of the founding fathers of the United States. Most of these men were 'deists'; in other words they did not deny the existence of God but rarely, if ever, attempted to pigeonhole the deity. The Foundation has never shown itself to be *against* Christianity – and in fact many of its workers across the years have been Christians. But neither does it restrict its efforts to promoting either the Christian religion or strictly Christian values – which has been enough to ensure criticism from lobbies that consider Christianity to be the only *true* belief and a religion that should ultimately be accepted by all citizens of the world. In addition, the Rockefeller Foundation actively supports branches of science that Christian fundamentalism would be happy to see abandoned – for example, the belief in evolution as opposed to creation.

David Rockefeller is accused of being part of a supposedly huge and well-choreographed plot that seeks to subvert individual nations' governments in favour of a 'one-world government', to which all of humanity will belong. Whether this is actually true or not, it *is* a fact that David Rockefeller donated the land upon which the United Nations building stands in New York – in order to ensure that the organization would have its headquarters in the United States, and not in Switzerland, as many people had suggested.

A brief perusal of the internet could easily lead uninformed readers to believe that David Rockefeller is the devil incarnate and that the Rockefeller Foundation is an institution deliberately created to subjugate humanity and to spiritually and even financially impoverish citizens of the world. It is certainly true that the Rockefeller Foundation gave financial sponsorship to the study of eugenics in the 1920s, a strange pseudoscience that dealt with supposedly improving the moral and physical stature of human beings. Eugenics was taken to horrific extremes in the dark science of Nazism, but in its initial incarnation it did no more than reflect some of the peculiar ideas that had predominated toward the end of the Victorian period. I am sure that those running the Rockefeller Foundation these days deeply regret their support of this field of research, which has been totally debunked and is quite rightly deplored these days.

There are plenty of internet sites shooting bullets at both David Rockefeller and the Rockefeller Foundation, but alas very few that point out just what has been achieved thanks to the philanthropy of the Rockefeller family. And of course none of this has anything to do with the possibility that the Rockefellers may have been used as a means of intervention from the future.

The problem with which we are faced is that we cannot know the political, moral or spiritual aspirations of our possibly distant future selves. It is quite telling that virtually all of those whose business it is to deal in popular science fiction – for example the writers of *Star Trek* – automatically accept that there will come a time when the Earth will have a 'world government'. Looking around ourselves right now, everything points in this direction. The United Nations takes a bigger and bigger role in policing the world and in introducing institutions and campaigns that are specifically geared toward internationalism. Bodies such as the European Union, which presently unites a great many of the countries of Western and Central Europe in an economic embrace, becomes more political with every passing year. Meanwhile, mutual military endeavours, such as those represented by NATO, gain new members all the time.

The old divisions of East and West have now broken down. Economically speaking, it is not presently in the interest of any nation to rock the world's boat, because all would suffer equally as a result. The old Communist bloc is now almost exclusively capitalistic in nature, and even China is utterly dependent on the goods and services it supplies to the West. Its ideology has had to change to compensate for its present role in the world and, as with so many other previously Communist regimes, its populace, except in the wholly agricultural areas, grows richer by the year.

As I pointed out in my last book *City of the Goddess – Washington DC*,[18] despite the direst prognostications of the prophets of doom that proliferate in the press, and especially on the internet, we presently live in the most peaceful era that humanity has ever known. True, there are still wars, such as the Gulf wars, the war in Afghanistan and the civil wars presently playing out across the Middle East, but these are tiny affairs in comparison with the wars of even the fairly recent past. So often those who have their own particular axe to grind fail to mention this – in fact, they almost never do. It is as if there is nothing interesting or newsworthy about the fact that, taken globally, humanity is now more educated, in better health and living longer than it has ever done. Certainly in the First World there is absolutely no comparison between the way we live and the lives of our grandparents and great-grandparents. Even poverty in the First World, though very real and to be deplored, does not imply what poverty meant a couple of generations ago.

Of course, there is still true poverty, injustice, starvation and untold horrors in the world, but it is not an idle boast to suggest that although we can always do better, we are presently doing more to address these blights than has ever been the case before.

One might therefore be forgiven for suggesting that if we are under the influence of people who want to manipulate the world – to subvert nationalism in favour of internationalism and to reduce us all to the level of automatons – we are not faring too badly across the board as a result. Of course, there are many exceptions but that is no reason to ignore the steps forward that have been taken. Does even the most diehard campaigner for the rights of humanity, the needs of the planet, and the supposed criminality of politicians and financiers, seriously want to go back to the days of soup kitchens and an education that finished at around 13 years of age?

It might not be palatable for some reason, and it is certainly not particularly PC to point out the fact, but the world is getting better by just about every definable measure. On the way toward a fairer, more equitable society there are going to be trials and turmoil – but how very far we have come since the days of feudal servitude. This has been possible in no short measure thanks to the people of vision who, even at the risk of their own lives, sought liberty and equality for all people, and who refused to allow religious power-groups and reactionary political models to get in the way.

Everything points to the fact that so many of these people have been influenced by an outside agency that could only be human influence from a point somewhere forward in time.

So much information is now pouring in, that we might look toward a period in the very near future when these facts will become known to all of us. Thus, for the last chapter of this book I want to concentrate on that event – when we will be confronted for the first time, openly and with no equivocation, with the people we are destined to become. I am certain that I already know *where* this will happen, it now only remains to work out *when*.

CHAPTER 14

On the White House Lawn

If you were to type 'Aliens on the White House Lawn' into Google, you would encounter nearly 13,000,000 possible entries. Sadly, it has been impossible to track down when this, or other versions of the statement, such as 'Aliens land on the White House Lawn' was first used. The phrase has become a metaphor and is much beloved of UFO believers – particularly since it could so easily have happened in 1952. As I pointed out earlier, on two occasions in 1952 unidentified flying objects were sighted hovering over Washington DC.

Actually the White House lawn would not be a very good place to land a UFO – at least not a really impressive one. Nothing bigger than about 50 metres across would fit! Better by far to land your UFO in Ellipse Park, just a little to the south. There you could park a giant spacecraft of 200 metres in diameter – even allowing for the National Christmas tree! And since the Ellipse is now officially known as President's Park, I suppose it is technically the White House Lawn.

Joking aside, where did this phrase come from? I suppose it suggests that the president of the United States is the most powerful individual in the world, and so anyone or anything wishing to converse with humanity as a whole would be likely to seek out the president as a natural representative of our species. It therefore seemed all the more appropriate, and of course slightly amusing, when we first discovered the huge and elaborate Megalithic arrow that points directly to the very centre of the Ellipse (*see* page 171). Erich von Däniken would be elated.

As I have pointed out, I for one do not accept that we are about to be visited any time soon by beings from elsewhere in the cosmos, but it is interesting to realize that this spot, at the very centre of Washington DC, has already been earmarked for some sort of 'first encounter' in the popular press, on film and television, to the extent that it has become fixed in our language.

In terms of intervention, I do not doubt for one moment that Washington DC as a whole was deliberately planned and created to be the focal point of humanity's first direct and unequivocal encounter with our future selves. Nor do I shy away from recognizing that when humanity eventually does respond to one overall governing body – hopefully of its own free will – that this will be based in Washington DC.

As I have shown time and again in our last five or six books, both alone and with Christopher Knight, the most important and significant city in the ancient world was undoubtedly Jerusalem. It is still considered as such by three of the world's major religions. On Medieval maps Jerusalem was invariably shown to be at the very centre of everything and was known as the 'navel of the world'. However, this state of affairs began to alter when Jerusalem was lost to Christianity after the long and bloody Crusades that had begun at the very end of the 11th century and which carried on for over two centuries.

Many researchers, including ourselves, believe that when that mysterious group of fighting monks, the Knights Templar, were silent to history and in Jerusalem between around 1119 and 1129, they were far from idle. Freemasonic tradition suggests, as does a wealth of writers, that they were busy digging under the foundations of the original Temple of Jerusalem, which is precisely where they were garrisoned by the king of Jerusalem, Baldwin II.

Again, according to Freemasonic tradition, what the Templars found there were artefacts that had been first buried beneath the Mound way back in time, even before the Hebrews came to control Jerusalem. Whatever had been placed there had been hidden by Enoch, a shadowy character from pre-Judaic times. More information on this topic is available in our previous books, particularly *The Hiram Key Revisited*[19] and *Before the Pyramids*.[20]

At least part of what the treasure seems to have been was a pedestal, with a triangular top. This was known as the 'Delta of Enoch'. (Delta is the fourth letter of the Greek alphabet and is triangular in shape.) This delta was made of pure gold, inlaid with precious stones. According to tradition, transcribed upon it was the ineffable name of God. The golden delta was then sunk into a block of agate and was hidden at the bottom of nine chambers, where it was eventually found by the much later King Solomon, who also located large columns left by Enoch upon which were engraved rudiments of all the arts and sciences from Enoch's time.

A lost book of the Old Testament, the Book of Enoch, was eventually rediscovered in Ethiopia and is now available to researchers. It details Enoch's life and his travels, which were extensive. In one section he travelled far to the north, to a structure that could only realistically have been the amazing site of Newgrange in Ireland. Enoch seems to have been of the same priestly class that was ultimately responsible for the greatest of the Megalithic structures of the world and it is highly likely that details of the Megalithic measuring system were included on the brass pillar that was eventually relocated and subsequently reburied by King Solomon.

Tradition asserts that these and other treasures were once more unearthed by the Knights Templar, and that they were transhipped to France – most likely to either Chartres or Troyes in Champagne. Since the Knights Templar were pronounced heretical in 1307, it would have been prudent to move the treasures out of France, to a location beyond the grasp of the avaricious King Philip II. Our research shows that they were initially taken to Kilwinning in Scotland, before being transferred to a building that had been specifically created for them. This was Rosslyn Chapel, near Edinburgh – one of the strangest and most enigmatic structures to be found anywhere in Europe.[21]

As demonstrated by Christopher Knight and Robert Lomas in their book *The Hiram Key*[22], Rosslyn Chapel, completed in the mid-15th century, is a copy of the Herodian temple in Jerusalem, which had been built on the foundations of Solomon's original temple. Deep below the foundations of Rosslyn Chapel, the Delta of Enoch and undoubtedly other treasures found by the Templars in Jerusalem were safeguarded for around 400 years.

The real objective of the Templars – and those who followed them once the order had been disbanded – was the creation of a 'New Jerusalem', which became more of a philosophical ideal than a religious one. Freemasonry was the true legatee of Templarism, and with its efforts the New Jerusalem found its form far to the west, in the new United States of America. It would be called Washington and would mark the final resting place of the treasures of Enoch.

Exactly when the treasures were removed from Rosslyn Chapel and transhipped to North America is difficult to say. It is possible that they originally went to Williamsburg, the old capital of the State of Virginia. There they were hidden temporarily beneath Bruton Parish Church – a place regularly visited by both George Washington and Thomas Jefferson prior to the American Declaration of Independence and the war that followed.

With the founding of Washington as the new capital of the free United States after 1788, the treasures were most probably moved from Virginia to an area of Washington still known to this day as Rosslyn. Their eventual home was intended to be at the very centre of Columbia, the district in which Washington itself stands. This did not become possible until after the American Civil War and so it was not until between 1877 and 1880 that the Ellipse was formally laid out. We know from the reports of Thomas Lincoln Casey, who was in charge of the operation, that whilst he was busy creating the Ellipse, the 'authorities' of Washington DC were busy digging a large hole at its centre, over which he had no jurisdiction or control. We can therefore say with some confidence that it was at this time that the treasures of Enoch finally found their present resting place, in a deliberately created chamber beneath the centre of Ellipse Park, which is, itself, at the very centre of the District of Columbia.

If we look again at the giant Megalithic arrow, that had been pointing the way to the centre of the Ellipse ever since Washington DC was first planned, it can be observed that if a line is drawn between Shaw Logan Circle and Dupont Circle, we have a triangle that includes the centre of the Ellipse in which all three sides conform to Megalithic proportions and which could easily be taken to represent the 'delta' of Enoch. So this is not simply an arrow pointing to the treasure but also a representation of the most important part of that treasure – the Delta of Enoch. There are also two other Megalithic triangles formed by the chevron.

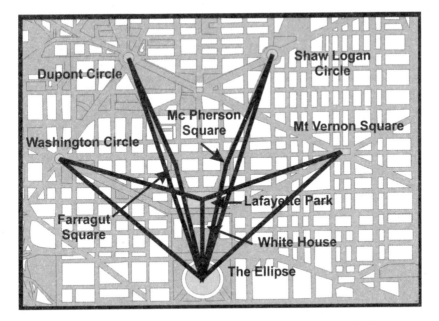

The Megalithic Arrow pointing to the centre of the Ellipse, which can also be seen as three separate triangles, all with Megalithic proportions.

All of this we have written about extensively, but what we have never been able to say with any certainty is exactly what the treasure of Enoch might tell us. It certainly represents an important 'bridge across time' connecting the remote period of the Neolithic with our own age. What is the 'ineffable name of God?' Does the brass pillar still exist and, if so, what could it tell us about the scientific knowledge that already existed 5,000 or more years ago – most likely as a legacy from the future?

Of the fact that *someone* knows there is no doubt. Megalithic measurements and geometry were used in the very planning of Washington DC and were still being used as recently as 1993 when the National World War II Memorial was planned and eventually placed on the Mall in Washington DC. The truth of these matters is undoubtedly in the hands of high-ranking Freemasons in Washington DC, who also hold influential and important roles across successive administrations.

Right now we can only guess what may have been deposited at the centre of Ellipse Park back in the 19th century. Logic suggests that it would represent a 'time capsule', the accumulated material of which would prove positively humanity's link with its own past – and future. The fact that the chamber and its contents remains hidden surely indicates that the time is not yet right for us to be in possession of this mind-boggling truth. There are presently too many divisions within humanity – especially religious ones. My guess is that the God of the future will be similar to that espoused by the deists such as George Washington and Thomas Jefferson. Neither of these men was irreligious, but as is the case with Freemasonry, they would not allow themselves to be committed to any specific creed. What they could not condone was the notion that any particular religion could be allowed to play a role in the running of any state. They both firmly believed that a man or woman's religious convictions were a matter for their own conscience. The sadder parts of human history are littered with the bones of those who fought and died to prove that *their* God was better or more real than the God of their neighbour.

It is a fact that political and economic differences across the world are gradually beginning to disappear. As creaky and even corrupt as it sometimes appears to be, the world is now more or less totally committed to capitalism. It is also increasingly committed to democracy. Dictatorships are gradually beginning to disappear and even nation-states that have never known anything but totalitarian rule are, as I write these words, making their bid for freedom and self-determination.

What lies before us is the greatest adventure humanity will ever know. Our conception of the way time works will have to change and, if my observations in the earlier parts of this book are correct, we will also have to come to terms with the fact that we are, in great measure, responsible for our own existence. Eventually we will come to the biggest challenge of all – the creation, 4.6 billion years ago, of Earth's Moon. Everything leads to this one major construction project, which will take the skill and ingenuity of humanity as a whole to address.

Long before this takes place we will have come to terms with the true nature of the past, present and future. Once the penny drops we must surely become different people, but the process cannot happen in a moment and neither will it be free from strife because some individuals, especially fundamentalist believers, will fight like fury to maintain the status quo. In a peculiar way that doesn't really matter because the battle is already won. I can walk out into my garden on almost any night and look up to see the serene face of the Moon looking back at me. We *will* succeed and humanity *must* put its prejudices behind it in order to seek a common goal. I do not say this because I am an eternal optimist but because the proof is already present.

The world is moving forward at an incredible pace. Information technology has played a great part in the striving for freedom that has been the hallmark of the last couple of years. I now, almost daily, not only talk to colleagues and readers in various parts of the world but I can see them, too – and it costs me nothing. This is science fiction made real. The sum total of human knowledge will very soon be available to anyone at the push of a few buttons. It is impossible under these circumstances for individuals or regimes, no matter how powerful, to control people in the way they have done far back through time. There is still some way to go and there will undoubtedly be setbacks because reactionary forces will not willingly let go of past prejudices. However, I estimate that we are much closer to fully realizing our own destiny, and our true past, than we might realize.

In amongst the clues that litter history, and especially within the configurations that have been left in Washington DC, I have searched for some verification of the era at which our future and present selves will meet openly. There is one series of numbers that occurs time and again, in relation to the position, size and orbital characteristics of the Moon. It shows itself in various forms but can be represented as 27322. Could this be a clue to a specific date? If we view the number as 27-3-22, we might take it to represent 27 March 2022.

Bearing in mind that the whole of this adventure, since the time our ancient ancestors began to first map the heavens, has been based on astronomy, it might be worth taking a peek at what the sky will look like on that Sunday morning. If we were to stand on the veranda of the dome of the Capitol in Washington DC early on 27 March 2022, we would see the Moon rise at 4:47am; 12 minutes later, red Mars would be on the horizon, followed within a minute by Venus, bright and resplendent as a morning star. These two bright planets, ancient representatives of men and women, will stand with the crescent Moon on the eastern horizon for about 15 minutes until, at 5:13am, Saturn will rise to join them. Just over an hour later, at 6:30am, Jupiter will rise, clear and piercing, followed 9 minutes later by the much fainter Neptune. Bright little Mercury will appear in the first rays of the rising Sun at 6:55 and at exactly 7:00am, the Sun will rise. It will cut the horizon just 3° north of due east, and if it were to be viewed from the Mall, by the time it rose over the dome of the Capitol its light would frame the statue of 'Freedom' that looks east from the pinnacle of the dome.

To have so many of the solar system's planets, including the Sun and the Moon, so close together is rare. Our ancient ancestors who believed in astrology would have deemed it to be extremely significant and very auspicious. It also seems entirely appropriate that the Moon will lead the procession on that morning.

Will this then be the day when the truth of our destiny will be made clear to us? Might we expect the ceremonial opening of the chamber below the centre of the Ellipse – or even a first public encounter with representatives of humanity from the future? In all honesty I cannot be certain. This date is only 11 years away as I write these words, but with the pace of change so evident in the world right now – a pace that is gathering all the time – it surely is not out of the question.

I am indeed an optimist and cannot deny the fact. However, as far as the world and humanity is concerned this is an optimism based on observation. Perhaps it is time to ignore the prophets of doom, who daily forecast our inevitable demise, and to take a look at what humanity has actually achieved recently. True, we have many problems, but together we are beginning to address them. We are developing a new respect for the planet that is our home, and beginning to face up to the many responsibilities that fall upon us as the most successful species the world has ever known.

No matter how difficult all of this may at first seem to be, with the change in paradigm that intervention brings, much of what has happened in our past makes infinitely more sense. What is more, so much that has appeared recently, especially in popular culture, seems to have been custom-made to prepare us for the revelation that is to come. Science fiction conditions us to even the most extraordinary possibilities, whilst the use of special effects in movies and on television presents these in a form that is ever more convincing and less artificial. All of this may be quite intentional and part of the natural progression that better fits us for the surprises that lie in store.

In closing, I do appreciate that the suggestions put forward in this book will take some swallowing, but I refer readers to the thought-provoking words of the geneticist and evolutionary biologist J B S Haldane. He once said:

I have no doubt that in reality the future will be vastly more surprising than anything I can imagine. My own suspicion is that the Universe is not only stranger than we suppose, but stranger than we 'can' suppose.

The Megalithic System Explained

Long before telescopes were invented, human beings were already showing an interest in astronomy. We are, by nature, a very inquisitive species and we want to know what makes everything work in the way it does, so this interest in the sky isn't all that surprising. In addition to simple curiosity, it was probably also important to understand the workings of the sky for another reason. The sky was where the gods lived, so understanding its workings and cycles probably seemed to bring one closer to understanding the minds of the gods.

There were also very practical reasons for understanding the patterns and movements of heavenly objects. The Sun, Moon and planets keep their own cycles, some of which are very important to farming communities, and also to cultures that rely on hunting, especially if migratory species are involved. With a good understanding of the patterns formed by the Sun it is possible to measure the year and to make note of what should be done and when. 'If Bison move north in March we want to move north, too, or there won't be anything to eat; and in any case, if we move north before them it should be possible to head them off at the pass!'

Similarly, if we plant our seeds at the wrong time they probably won't grow at all, and a variety of other jobs associated with agriculture are dependent on knowing what the time of year actually is.

It seems to have been a very long time ago when it occurred to someone that the replicating patterns of the day and night fitted a certain number of times into the replicating patterns of the year. They didn't need to know that the Earth is spinning on its own axis, or that it was also travelling around the Sun. All they had to do was to watch what happened over their heads and to be able to measure and memorize the patterns involved.

Working out the number of days in a year wouldn't have been all that easy using the Sun. This is because it is so bright and because of its movements along the eastern horizon throughout the year. As the Sun gets to its extremes of north and south it slows down significantly, and for some days it appears to rise in almost exactly the same place; so which of these sunrises marks the end of one year and the beginning of another?

Stars are more obliging and will pop up in the same place on the horizon night after night. The only time they can't be seen is if they stay below the horizon during certain seasons, but stars that rise high into the sky will be visible throughout the year (except when the Sun is in the same part of the sky for two or three months).

Henges, such as the ones at Thornborough in Yorkshire, England, were built with this need partly in mind. There, the gap in the henges to the southwest was deliberately placed very close to where the star Sirius rose each night, but where the Sun also rose at the very time of its most southerly rising (the winter solstice).

It is a consequence of the Earth travelling around the Sun, and maintaining a particular angle relative to the Sun, that makes the Sun appear to rise and set on different parts of the horizon throughout the year. In the northern hemisphere the Sun rises well north of east in summer and well south of east during the winter months. When seen from Thornborough around 3500BC it never travelled any further south than the southwest henge entrances, and this was the position it achieved on the day of the midwinter solstice (the shortest day).

Those keeping the observations at Thornborough knew full well that by the time the Sun travelled north from its rising in the southwestern gaps, and then returned again, Sirius would have risen in the same gap 366 times. This told them there were 366 days in a year. This is a star year and is not the same as a solar year.

As far as the observer is concerned it amounts to this. A solar year is just over 365.25 days in length but, during the same time, a star will have risen 366 times. It sounds odd but it's true. Each day, according to the rising of a star (a sidereal day), is 23 hours 56 minutes 4 seconds in length, whereas an average solar day is 24 hours in length. That leaves a discrepancy of 236 seconds, which over a year amounts to almost exactly 24 hours. It is part of the clockwork mechanism of our solar system that there are different sorts of years, dependent on what one is observing. Our Megalithic and pre-Megalithic ancestors in Britain focused on the number of times a star rose in a year, and the result was 366 times.

Having made this realization, what they did next is the most surprising aspect of our studies across the last two decades. They created an integrated measuring system based upon a year of 366 days. Just as surely as they recognized the year could be split into 366 units, they also split the sky into 366 units, which we would know as degrees of arc. They then split the units again, first into minutes of arc. They considered that there were 60 minutes of arc to 1 degree of arc.

But this wasn't enough for them so they split the units again. Each minute of arc was split into 6 smaller units, which we would know as seconds of arc (note the difference between this form of geometry and the one we use now. In 360-degree geometry there are 60 seconds of arc to 1 minute of arc but in the Megalithic system there are only 6.)

Somehow they worked out that if they split the degree, minute and second of arc in this way, they would arrive at a stunning result. They reasoned that if the sky was a great circle, the size and shape of the Earth must just be the same circle turned inside out. In other words, if you could split the sky into

366 units, you could split the surface of the Earth in the same way. And when they did this the Megalithic second of arc of the polar Earth measured *exactly* 366 Megalithic Yards.

The actual size of the Megalithic Yard could be judged by the careful use of a pendulum of exactly half this length. At first this may have been used in conjunction with the Sun, but later a more sophisticated method was established using the planet Venus during certain parts of its orbit.

What is absolutely incredible about the Megalithic Yard as a unit of length, is not just that it is geodetic (fits into the polar circumference of the Earth in a logical and obviously intended way), but it does the same job on the Moon and the Sun. One Megalithic second of arc on the Moon measures exactly 100 Megalithic Yards. On the Sun the same Megalithic second of arc is 40,000 Megalithic Yards.

Getting the sheer genius of this system across to our readers has been the hardest part of our quest because it really is incredible, but it can seem complicated. Once the penny drops, the whole system is virtually miraculous. In this system a second of arc of the sky can be seen as the same thing as a second of time of the Earth turning on its axis. In other words 1 Megalithic second of the Earth turning on its axis also represents a physical segment of the sky, albeit an extremely small one because it is 1/366th of 1/360th of the sky. The same second is also a finite measurement of part of the Earth's circumference. Time, geometry and distance all merge into the same symmetrical whole, and astronomical calculations become much easier.

Meanwhile, with the system we use today we have degrees, minutes and seconds of arc of the sky, and of the circumference of our planet. We also have minutes and seconds of time but these don't match the turning sky at all. This fact must have cost thousands of human lives as the first mariners to engage in transatlantic voyages tried desperately to reconcile minutes and seconds of time with minutes and seconds of geometrical arc and came up with the wrong answer.

We eventually discovered that, in addition to measuring time and linear distance, the Megalithic system had also been based on the mass of the Earth. How could this possibly be? It's absurd, and yet it is self-evidently true. The unit of mass in question is virtually the same as the unit presently known as the imperial pound. The mass of the Earth is 5.9742 x 10^{24} kilograms. In pounds this figure is 1.31708565 x 10^{25} pounds. With just a very slight change in the definition of the pound, this figure becomes 1.317600 x 10^{25} pounds and then something amazing happens. Imagine we segment the Earth like an orange. A segment 1 Megalithic second of arc across would have a mass of exactly 1 x 10^{20} pounds. That's 100,000,000,000,000,000,000 pounds!

This means that the imperial pound and the pound that was a part of the Megalithic system are virtually identical. The Megalithic pound had a value of 99.96 per cent of the modern pound! The difference is 0.4 of a gram. That this level of accuracy has been maintained across such a vast period of time is little short of incredible.

In order to turn the Megalithic Yard into a system for measuring volume and mass we need to resort to the Megalithic Inch. Alexander Thom found this unit when he carefully studied carvings that had been scratched into a number of standing stones. He established that there had been 40 Megalithic Inches to 1 Megalithic Yard. A cube with sides of 1/10th of a Megalithic Yard (4 Megalithic Inches) holds the same as a modern pint of water. If the water is poured out and the same cube is filled with any cereal grain, such as wheat, barley or even un-hulled rice, the weight of the cereal grain will be one pound.

So what do we have?

The Megalithic system is a system of geometry and measurement that is based upon a 366-day year, together with the physical size and mass of the Earth. It measures time, distance, mass and volume using the same figures throughout, and aspects of it are as relevant to the Moon and Sun as they are here on Earth. Without wishing to detract from our stunning scientific accomplishments as a species, anyone would surely have to admit that the Megalithic system is better in a number of ways than any method of measurement used today. This is because it is *integrated* and because a common terminology is used throughout. The metric system in use today may be extremely accurate and it, too, was originally based on the circumference of the Earth, but it certainly does not take Earth mass into account and neither is it used for the measurement of time.

Unbelievable as it may seem, thanks to our friend and colleague Edmund Sixsmith we now believe that the Megalithic system also dealt with the measurement of temperature. If we create a temperature scale in which the freezing point of water is 0° Megalithic and the boiling point of water is 366° Megalithic, something quite magical happens. Absolute zero, the lowest temperature achievable (usually considered to be -273.15°C) becomes an absolutely round and quite accurate -1,000° Megalithic.

Since there is little chance that our Megalithic ancestors were interested in measuring temperatures, let alone be in possession of the technology to do so, the Megalithic temperature system stands as proof that as ingenious and useable as aspects of the Megalithic system were to our ancient ancestors, they did not create it. Rather they must have 'inherited' it from a previous technological culture that is now lost to us – or more likely from our future ancestors.

The Message in Detail²³

T he message that we have detected is present in reoccurring number sequences that are frequently round numbers. The starting point of recognizing that something highly unusual was happening was when we discovered that the Megalithic system of geometry worked on the Moon and the Sun as well as the Earth.

Looking into issues concerning the Moon we were immediately reminded of the strange coincidence that the Moon and the Sun appear to be the same size in Earth's skies, leading to the phenomenon we call a total eclipse. Still stranger is the fact that the relation is so numerically neat, with the Moon being 400 times smaller than the Sun and 400 times closer to the Earth at the point of a total eclipse. On its own this could be a bizarre coincidence but because of what follows we believe that it is the *headline* to a message built into the Moon 4.6 billion years ago.

The Megalithic System

The Megalithic system of geometry is based on 366 degrees to a circle, 60 minutes to a degree and 6 seconds to a minute. This sequence produces a second of arc on the Earth's polar circumference that is 366 Megalithic Yards long – the linear measure of the Megalithic builders as identified by Alexander Thom.

As a cross-reference we had also discovered that the 4,000-year-old

Minoan Foot is precisely equal to a 1,000th part of a Megalithic second of arc.

We applied the principles of Megalithic geometry to all of the planets and Moons in the solar system and found that it only produced round integer results for the Sun and the Moon. The Sun is very close to being a true sphere, certainly much more so than the Earth. NASA quote the mean volumetric circumference as being 4,373,096km, which we converted into Megalithic Yards and applied the 366 geometry.

Sun's circumference	=	5,270,913,968 MY
One degree	=	14,401,404 MY
One minute	=	240,023 MY
One second	=	40,003.8 MY

The fit is 99.99 per cent accurate to 40,000 MY and given that this is based on a best estimate of the mean circumference, it has to be considered bang on.

Like the Sun, the Moon is quite close to being a sphere. NASA gives the mean volumetric circumference of 10,914.5km, which produces the following result:

Moon's circumference	=	13,155,300 MY
One degree	=	35,943 MY
One minute	=	599 MY
One second	=	99.83 MY

If we use the equatorial radius the result is 99.9 MY per second of lunar arc. Either way this is as close to 100 MY as makes no difference given the irregular surface of the Moon and the small variation in Thom's definition of the Megalithic Yard of +/- 0.061cm.

It could have been possible for people many thousands of years ago to create a system of geometry that produces round integers for two celestial objects such as the Earth and the Sun, but it would seem impossible to achieve such a feat for three bodies. It therefore appears that the Moon was designed using units derived from the physical dimensions of the Sun and the Earth.

The Earth – Moon Relationship

The duration of the Moon's orbit (sidereal – fixed star to fixed star) is 27.322 Earth days (27.396 rotations of the Earth). This number is extraordinarily close to the size relationship of the Moon to the Earth, being 27.31 per cent of the Earth's size.

The Earth currently turns on its axis 366.259 times for each orbit around the Sun. This number is extraordinarily close to the size relationship of the Earth to the Moon, being 366.175 per cent larger than the Moon.

There is no reason why these numbers should repeat in this way:

Earth turns per orbit   % size of polar
                                               circumference

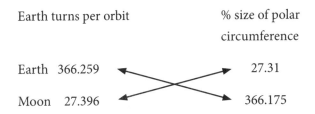

Earth 366.259   27.31

Moon   27.396   366.175

It is also a consequence of the above that the Moon makes 366 orbits of the Earth in 10,000 Earth days.

The sizes of the Sun, Earth and Moon have been fixed for billions of years so their size ratios have not changed. But the orbital characteristics of the Earth and the Moon have changed constantly.

When the Moon was much closer to the Earth than it is now, its orbit was much shorter and the Earth day was also shorter, leading to perhaps as many as 600 days to the Earth year. The Earth's own orbit around the Sun remains essentially unchanged. It is only the time it takes to spin on its own axis that alters.

The close number association between the size ratios of the Sun, Moon and Earth, and the orbital characteristics of the Moon, together with the present length of the Earth day, are only applicable to the time that humans have been fully formed. These relationships were not present in the distant past and they will disappear in the distant future. The number sequences that alerted us to the 'message' are clearly meant for the present period.

The Metric System

Orbital characteristics and size relationships are physical factors and any correlations are real – no matter what units of measurement are employed. No one knows the origin of the Megalithic system, but the origin of the metric system is fully documented. Whilst it did have a near identical precursor in the Sumerian system of more than 4,000 years earlier, the metric system has been developed from measuring the polar circumference of the Earth alone.

It was designed so that there should be 40,000km in one Earth circumference. The equator is a little longer than the polar circumference but basically the Earth turns through this distance each day.

The Moon turns through in an unimpressive sounding 10,920.8 kilometres every 27.3217 days. This converts to 400km per Earth day – to accuracy greater than 99.9 per cent. Again, this is a factor that only exists in the human period of existence.

The number 400 is already central to human appreciation of the Moon because it is 400 times closer to us than the Sun and it is 400 times smaller. The use of 400 kilometres per current Earth day could be a message that the architect of the Moon knew we would use kilometres and mean solar days.

Metric units apart, the Moon is turning at a rate that is almost exactly 1 per cent of the Earth's rotation. Or to reverse the factor, the Earth is turning 100 times as fast as the Moon. All curiously round values!

To add to the idea that this is a deliberate piece of metric design, the Moon is also travelling on its journey around the Earth at a steady rate of 1 kilometre per second! This speed varies a little as it travels but does not drop below 0.964km per second and does not exceed 1.076km per second.

And there is something else very special about the kilometre as regards the Moon. To understand it we need to realize that there are 109.2 Earth diameters across the Sun's diameter. There are also 109.2 Sun diameters between the Earth and the Sun at its furthest point of orbit.

The circumference of the Moon is 109.2 x 100 kilometres.

Is that not odd in the extreme?

One way of looking at the association between these ratios and numbers can be seen in the diagram overleaf.

There are many factors here that should bear no relationship with each other at all. Taken in isolation, any one of these strange associations might be considered to be a coincidence, but there comes a time when coincidences become so frequent that it is obvious that something else is at work.

366
The number of rotations in an Earth year

366
The number of Megalithic Yards in 1 Mg second of arc of the Earth

366%
The percentage size Moon to Earth

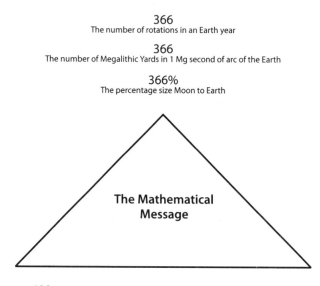

**The Mathematical
Message**

400
The ratio of the size of the Moon
to that of the Sun

1/400th
The number of times the Moon is
closer to the Earth than the Sun

40,000
The number of Megalithic Yards in
1 Mg second of arc of the Sun

40,000
The number of kilometres the Earth
turns on its axis in a day

400
The number of kilometres the Moon
turns on its axis in a day

10,000
The number of days in 366
lunar orbits

100
The number of Megalithic Yards in 1 Mg
second of arc of the Moon

400
The number of times the Earth
rotates faster than the Moon

109.28
The ratio of the size of the Earth
to that of the Sun

109.25
The number of Earth diameters
across the diameter of the Sun

109.26
The number of solar diameters
across the Earth's orbit at aphelion

27.322
The sidereal days in 1 lunar orbit
27.322 X 4 = 109.2

27.322%
The percentage size Earth to Moon

10,920.8
The size of the Moon in kilometres

Endnotes

1 *See Before the Pyramids*, Christopher Knight and Alan Butler, Watkins, 2010

2 *The Aliens and the Scalpel*, Leir, Dr R, Book Tree, US, 2005

3 *See* Appendix 1

4 The pint is still used in many parts of the world. In most areas it has been superseded by metric measurements but the United States retains it in daily use. Although Britain has adopted the metric system, the pint is also commonly used here.

5 Like the pint, the avoirdupois pound is still commonly used throughout the world.

6 I am indebted to Edmund Sixsmith for this realization.

7 A weight of 1,000lb is half of the 'short ton' still used in the United States and often referred to there simply as 1 ton.

8 *See Civilization One.*

9 Definitely not side by side as grains were used for measurement in more recent centuries in Europe.

10 *Astronomy – A Dictionary of Space and the Universe*, Iain Nicholson, Arrow Books, 1977

11 *Who Built the Moon?* Christopher Knight and Alan Butler, Watkins, 2005

12 A Megalithic Rod is a unit also rediscovered by Prof. Alexander Thom; it is 2.5 Megalithic Yards in length.

13 *The Goddess, the Grail and the Lodge*, Alan Butler, O Books, 2003

14 *Sheep*, Alan Butler, O Books, 2010

15 *The Goddess, the Grail and the Lodge*, Alan Butler, O Books, 2003

16 *The Hiram Key Revisited*, Christopher Knight and Alan Butler, Watkins, 2010

[17] *Dr Thorne*, Anthony Trollope, Everyman edition, 1993, first published 1858

[18] *City of the Goddess – Washington DC*, Alan Butler, Watkins Publishing, 2011

[19] *The Hiram Key Revisited*, Christopher Knight and Alan Butler, Watkins, 2010

[20] *Before the Pyramids*, Christopher Knight and Alan Butler, Watkins, 2009

[21] *Rosslyn Revealed*, Alan Butler and John Ritchie, O Books, 2006

[22] *The Hiram Key*, Christopher Knight and Robert Lomas, Century, 1996

[23] Reproduced from *Who Built the Moon?* by Christopher Knight and Alan Butler, Watkins, 2005

Index

physics 28–30, 78
technical problems of 21
time loops 28, 29
see also linear nature of time
treasures of Enoch 168–72
Trilateral Commission 162
trilithons 2
Trollope, Anthony 161–2
Troyes 98, 150, 154, 155, 156

UFOs (Unidentified Flying Objects)
accounts of 65–6, 67–8
Alan Butler's experience of 83–4
Bridlington Bay, sightings from 63–4
conspiracy theories 66–7
explanations of 62, 63, 64–5, 68–70
Rendlesham Forest, sightings at 59–62
surveillance by 69
visits from the future 70–2
see also alien intervention
underworld 104, 105
Unidentified Flying Objects (UFOs)
see UFOs
Unidentified Submerged Objects (USOs)
see USOs
United Airlines Flight 93 146
United Nations 164, 165
United States
9/11 attacks *see* 9/11 attacks
Freemasons *see* Freemasons
liberty 158–9
Megalitihic measuring system 81, 96,
131–3 *see also* Ellipse Park
religion 159, 160, 163–4, 172
see also Washington DC
United States Naval Observatory 131
USOs (Unidentified Submerged Objects)
67–8, 69

van Stockum, Willem 29, 30
Venus
association with goddess Inanna 103–4
composition of 119, 120
Megalithic Yard and double kush 113–14
phases 104
Sumerian pendulum experiment 103, 105,
108
transition from morning to evening star 105
Victoria (sailing ship) 67
visits from the future *see* travelling back in
time
von Däniken, Erich
alien intervention vii–viii, ix, 10–12
gaffs 11
mythical gods viii, 11

Washington DC
9/11 attacks *see* 9/11 attacks
Ellipse Park *see* Ellipse Park
henge discovery 131
Megalithic measuring system 131–4, 136–7,
172
military base 136
new meridian 135
Pentagon *see* Pentagon
planning and building of 82, 131–3
treasures of Enoch 168–72
UFOs 65–6, 69
see also Jefferson, Thomas
Watson, Lyall 37
White, Tim 46
Who Built the Moon? 122, 123, 124
Wolpoff, Milford 53, 54
Wood, John 128–9, 130
wool 153, 155–6, 158
world government 140, 162, 164–5
World Trade Centre 139, 143, 146, 147